Acol Bridge for Bright Improvers

All lively-minded players, keen for a rapid
improvement in their game, will welcome this
excellent sequel to *Acol Bridge for Bright Beginners*.
Here the authors cover more advanced bidding
techniques and the development of bidding
judgement, and then give detailed advice on those
sophisticated card-play skills that turn potentially
losing contracts into winners. Every chapter has its
own follow-up quiz.

English Bridge said of *Acol Bridge for Bright
Beginners*: 'It is the latest in a long line of excellent,
readable books from the Master Bridge Series. It
comes with the authority and gravitas of the late Hugh
Kelsey, international player, writer and a leading
world authority on bridge, and Britain's leading
teacher and great communicator, Andrew Kambites.'

ACOL BRIDGE *for* BRIGHT IMPROVERS

Hugh Kelsey & Andrew Kambites

VICTOR GOLLANCZ
in association with
PETER CRAWLEY

First published in Great Britain 1996
in association with Peter Crawley
by Victor Gollancz
An imprint of the Cassell Group
Wellington House, 125 Strand, London WC2R 0BB

A catalogue record for this book
is available from the British Library

ISBN 0 575 06317 3

Photoset in Great Britain by
Rowland Phototypesetting Limited, Bury St Edmunds, Suffolk.
Printed in Great Britain by
St Edmundsbury Press Limited, Bury St Edmunds, Suffolk.

Contents

Introduction

To any ambitious bridge author there could have been no greater compliment than an invitation to collaborate with Hugh Kelsey. The project was exciting too: two books aimed at showing the reader how to think rather than just giving a list of instructions. For many years Hugh was the acknowledged inspiration of so many of Britain's experts. I can remember as a keen improver reading Hugh's classic *Killing Defence at Bridge* and deciding that bridge offered more of an intellectual challenge than I had realised. Hugh was the expert's expert.

Our first book, *Acol Bridge for Bright Beginners*, proceeded without hitch. Sadly Hugh's health was far from good and the completion of *Acol Bridge for Bright Improvers* was interrupted by his death, leaving me with the responsibility for its completion. I can only hope that the master would have approved of the final text. I am grateful to Hugh's widow, Flora, for enthusiasm that our project be completed.

Acol Bridge for Bright Improvers assumes you have reasonable understanding of the material contained in a book for beginners. If you know nothing about bridge obviously I would recommend that you start with *Acol Bridge for Bright Beginners*. If you master the contents of this book you should be far stronger than most social players, and capable of holding your own in any bridge club. Hopefully, by then you will be well on the way to becoming an expert.

Andrew Kambites

1. Summary of the Basic Acol Bidding Structure

Classification of Bids

If you have been taught bridge, or taught yourself by means of a beginners' book you will have realised that bids fall into various classifications. In order to improve your bridge it is important that you understand the classification, rather than just memorise a point-count. When we discuss bidding we refer to the appropriate classification with the abbreviations listed below.

[L]   Limit bid. A bid that defines the bidder's values very closely, usually allowing his partner to make a quick decision as to the final contract.

[WR] Wide-ranging bid. The bidder's values could lie within a wide range.

[F]   Forcing bid, requiring partner to find another bid (unless the opposition intervene).

[F1R] Forcing bid for one round only.

[GF] Game-forcing bid. The partnership mustn't allow the bidding to die until a game contract is reached.

[NF] Not forcing. Partner doesn't have to bid (but can choose to do so if he wishes).

[S]   Sign-off bid. Partner must not bid again.

[I]   Invitational bid. Partner is invited to proceed to game if he has maximum values within the limits he has already shown.

[C]   Conventional bid, not promising anything in the suit bid and therefore, by common sense, forcing.

The Acol Bidding System

As opener you should classify your hand as *balanced* or *unbalanced*. A balanced hand has shape 4–3–3–3, 4–4–3–2, or sometimes 5–3–3–2. All other hands are unbalanced and with the exception of 4–4–4–1 shape hands have at least one 5-card suit.

HCP refers to high-card points, 4 for an ace, 3 for a king, 2 for a queen and one for a jack. Points include length points: 1 for a

5-card suit, 2 for a 6-card suit etc. When supporting partner length points are discounted. Instead shortage points in the side suits are counted: one for a doubleton, 3 for a singleton and 5 for a void.

The Opening Bid

A balanced hand should aim to either open 1NT or open a suit bid and rebid no-trumps if partner changes suit [F].

12–14 HCP. Open 1NT [L].

15–16 HCP. Open a suit. Rebid no-trumps at the lowest legal level [L] if partner changes suit.

17–18 HCP. Open a suit. Rebid no-trumps with a jump [L] if partner changes suit.

19   HCP. Open a suit. Rebid 3NT [L].

20–22 HCP. Open 2NT [L].

23–24 HCP. Open 2♣ [C] and rebid 2NT [NF] over the negative 2◇ [C] response.

25–26 HCP. Open 2♣ [C] and rebid 3NT [NF] over 2◇ [C].

An unbalanced hand should open its longest suit. If partner changes suit [F] show a second suit or rebid your suit.

Responding to 1NT

2♣ [C]   The Stayman Convention (see chapter 2).

2◇/2♡/2♠ [S]   0–10 points and a 5-card or longer suit.

2NT [I]   Shows 11–12 points and asks opener to pass with a minimum 1NT opening or raise to 3NT with a maximum.

3♣/3◇ [GF]   Slam try. Opener raises the suit with support or rebids 3NT [NF] without support.

3♡/3♠ [GF]   Usually 5 cards in the bid suit. Opener is required to rebid 3NT with only doubleton support, or raise to 4♡/4♠ with 3-card or 4-card support.

3NT [S]   13–19 HCP, with no 5-card major suit.

4♡/4♠/5♣/5◇ [S]   Shows at least a 6-card suit.

4NT [I]   Shows 20 points and asks opener to pass with a minimum 1NT opening or raise to 6NT with a maximum.

Slams [S].   To play.

Responding to a Suit Bid (e.g., 1♡ [WR])

2♡ [L]   A single raise shows 6–9 points + 4-card support (but see page 35 for more sophisticated treatment).

3♡ [L]   A double raise shows 10–12 points + 4-card support.

4♡ [L]   A triple raise shows 13–15 points + 4-card support (but see page 44 for more sophisticated treatment).

1NT [L]   6–9 HCP (8–10 if the opening bid was 1♣).

2NT [L]   11–12 HCP, balanced.

3NT [L]   13–15 HCP, balanced.

1♠ [F]   A one-level change of suit shows 6+ points.

2♣ [F]   A two-level change of suit without a jump shows 8+ HCP.

2♠ [GF]   A jump in a new suit shows 16+ points and a good quality suit (at least 5 cards).

Opener's Rebid with an Unbalanced Hand

After a change of suit at the one-level, e.g., 1♡ 1♠:

2♠ [L]   A single raise shows 12–15 points + 4-card support.

3♠ [L]   A double raise shows 16–18 points + 4-card support.

4♠ [L]   A triple raise shows 19+ points + 4-card support.

2♡ [L]   Opener rebids his suit at the cheapest level to show 12–15 points and at least a 5-card suit.

3♡ [L]   Opener rebids his suit with a jump to show 16–18 points and at least a strong 6-card suit.

4♡ [L]   Opener rebids his suit at game level to show 19–20 points and a strong suit, usually at least 7 cards.

2♢ [WR] [NF]   Opener bids a third suit without a jump to show 12–18 points.

3♢ [GF]   Opener bids a third suit with a jump to show 19+ points.

After a change of suit at the two-level, e.g., 1♡ 2♣ the rebids are the same unless you support partner.

3♣ [L]   A single raise shows 12–16 points + 4-card support.

4♣ [L]   A double raise shows 17+ points + 4-card support (but see page 26 for more sophisticated treatment).

Note that 1♠ 2♡ promises at least 5 hearts so opener should support hearts with just 3-card support.

Strong Opening Bids

2◇/2♡/2♠ [F1R]. Acol two-bids promise an excellent suit and
at least 8 tricks if partner has nothing. The negative
response is 2NT [C] showing 0–7 HCP. All other responses are game-forcing.

2♣ [C] shows 23+ points. It is game-forcing unless the response
is the negative 2◇ [C] showing 0–7 HCP and opener's
rebid is 2NT [L] showing 23–24 HCP.

Pre-emptive Opening Bids

3♣/3◇/3♡/3♠ are pre-emptive opening bids, showing a weak
hand (below normal opening values) and a good quality suit,
usually 7 cards in length. If not vulnerable you should expect to
take 6 tricks if partner is worthless, if vulnerable you need 7
tricks.

If the enemy open a 3-level pre-empt, double is for takeout and
3NT shows 16–25 points with at least one stopper in their suit.

4♣/4◇/4♡/4♠ are pre-emptive opening bids, showing usually
at least a good 8-card suit, expecting to take 7 tricks if not
vulnerable or 8 if vulnerable.

Slam Bidding Conventions

After you have agreed a trump suit you can enquire how many
aces partner has with the Blackwood 4NT [C] convention. The
responses are:

5♣ [C] = 0 or 4 aces.   5◇ [C] = 1 ace.
5♡ [C] = 2 aces.   5♠ [C] = 3 aces.

After Blackwood 4NT you can sign off in the agreed trump suit at
the five, six or seven level.

Alternatively you can continue with 5NT [C] asking how many
kings partner has. The responses are:

6♣ [C] = 0 king.   6◇ [C] = 1 king.
6♡ [C] = 2 kings.   6♠ [C] = 3 kings.

After you have agreed a trump suit the bid of another suit is a
cue bid [C] showing first round control in that suit (the ace or a
void) and invites partner to co-operate in investigating a slam.

Bidding after the Enemy Opens the Bidding

For instance, over an opponent's 1♡ opening bid:

1♠ [WR] A one-level overcall shows 5+ spades and 9–16 points.
1NT [L] shows 16–18 balanced HCP, with a heart stopper.
2♣/2◇ [WR] A 2-level overcall without a jump shows 11–18 points and a 6-card or longer suit (perhaps 5 if the suit is very strong).
2♠/3♣/3◇ [NF] An overcall with a jump shows 16–19 points and a very strong suit (at least 6 cards).
3♠/4♣/4◇/4♠/5♣/5◇ are pre-emptive, showing a playing strength within three tricks of your bid if not vulnerable or within two tricks if vulnerable.
Double [C] is for take-out, suggesting shortage in their suit and asking partner to bid his best suit.

Responding to a Simple Suit Overcall

If partner overcalls in a suit you only need 3 trumps to support him. The overcall has a lower range than an opening bid so you needn't bid with 6 points or fewer.
e.g., if partner overcalls 1♡ with 1♠:
2♠ [L] = 8–10 points.
3♠ [L] = 11–13 points.
4♠ [S] = 14+ points, or a hand that expects to make the contract because of distributional values.

Responding to a Take-out Double

A double is for take-out if it is the double of a suit contract, at the 3-level or below and partner has done no more than say 'no bid'. Other doubles are for penalty.
   If partner doubles the enemy opening 1♡ for take-out and the next hand passes you must bid. Reply as follows:
1♠/2♣/2◇ = 0–7 points. Usually 4-card or longer suit, but since you must bid and you cannot bid their suit to play you might have to improvise with a 3-card suit.
1NT [L] = 6–10 HCP and at least one stopper in their suit.
2♠/3♣/3◇ = 8–12 points. At least 4 cards in the suit.
2NT [L] = 11–12 HCP and at least one stopper in their suit.
3NT [L] = 13–15 HCP and at least one stopper in their suit.

2. The Stayman Convention

It is usually desirable to uncover an 8-card major suit fit. It tends to be less important to play in such a minor suit fit because game in 5♣ or 5◇ requires 11 tricks. Such hands are frequently played in 3NT. The *Stayman* convention replaces the use of a 2♣ response to 1NT as a sign-off, with an enquiry bid to uncover a 4–4 major suit fit.

After a 1NT opening responder bids 2♣ [C] which demands that opener rebids his cheapest 4-card major (or 2◇ [C] if he hasn't got one). Responder guarantees that he himself holds at least one 4-card major and he must be satisfied that he can see a sensible resting place whatever opener rebids. This usually, though not always, means at least 11 points because if he fails to locate his required fit he will have to retreat to 2NT [I] (which shows the same 11–12 points as a direct raise of 1NT to 2NT).

Here are some Stayman sequences:

(a)

WEST	EAST	WEST	EAST
♠ K Q 4 2	♠ A 8	1NT	2♣
♡ A Q	♡ K J 6 5	2♠ (1)	2NT (2)
◇ 10 7 6	◇ A 9 8 2	3NT (3)	No
♣ K 7 4 2	♣ 8 6 3		

(1) Denies 4 hearts, shows 4 spades.
(2) 11–12 points, invitational. East must have 4 hearts or he wouldn't have enquired with 2♣.
(3) Maximum no trump-opening.

(b)

WEST	EAST	WEST	EAST
♠ Q J 4 2	♠ K 8 6 5	1NT	2♣
♡ Q J 4 2	♡ K 6	2♡ (1)	2NT (2)
◇ A 10 2	◇ K Q 7 3	4♠ (3)	No
♣ A 7	♣ 9 4 2		

(1) Shows 4 hearts, doesn't deny 4 spades.
(2) 11–12 points. No interest in hearts.
(3) West knows East has a 4-card major to bid Stayman. Since he doesn't like hearts he must have spades. With 14 points he accepts East's game try and jumps to 4♠.

(c)

WEST	EAST	WEST	EAST
♠ K 6 3	♠ Q 9 7 4 2	1NT	2♣ (1)
♡ A 5 4	♡ K 6 3 2	2◇ (2)	2♠ (3)
◇ A Q 7	◇ 10 4	No	
♣ 9 8 3 2	♣ 7 4		

(1) A rare occasion where it is safe to bid Stayman with a weak hand. East has thought out all the consequences. If West rebids 2♡ or 2♠ he will pass. If West rebids 2◇, denying a 4-card major, he will sign off in 2♠.

(2) Denies 4 hearts or 4 spades.

(3) A sign-off. This will be either a 5–3 or 5–2 fit.

If opener's hand is balanced he might have to bid 1NT when he has a weak doubleton. This increases the responsibility on responder to seek out the 4–4 major fit with Stayman if he has a 4-card major and sufficient values to invite game.

(d)

WEST	EAST	WEST	EAST
♠ A 10 9 2	♠ K 6 4 3	1NT	2♣
♡ K J 5 3	♡ Q 7 2	2♡	3NT
◇ 9 4	◇ A 5 2	4♠	
♣ K Q 4	♣ A 9 8		

You won't find universal agreement about whether East, whose shape is perfectly balanced, should immediately jump to 3NT over 1NT, or use Stayman to investigate the possibility of a spade fit. However, on this hand it is clear that 3NT is somewhat precarious on a diamond lead. The point is that although East doesn't seem to have a weakness, West might have one. The partners have different roles. Opener shows his hand character, in this case balanced. Responder looks for the 4–4 major fit.

Quiz 1

1) How do you respond to partner's 1NT with these hands?

(a)   ♠ A 8 3 2
      ♡ 4 3
      ◇ K J 4 2
      ♣ 10 4 3

(b)   ♠ A 8 3 2
      ♡ 4
      ◇ K J 9 4 2
      ♣ 10 4 3

(c)   ♠ A 8 3 2
      ♡ 10 9 4 3
      ◇ K J 9 4 2
      ♣ –

(d)   ♠ A 8 3 2
      ♡ Q 7 4 2
      ◇ J 10 6 5
      ♣ 3

(e)   ♠ J 8 3 2
      ♡ Q J 9 4 2
      ◇ K 7 2
      ♣ 3

(f)   ♠ A 8 4 3
      ♡ K 10
      ◇ K 10
      ♣ J 9 8 7 3

(g)   ♠ K Q 8 6 4
      ♡ 7 2
      ◇ A J 7
      ♣ A 10 9

(h)   ♠ K Q 8 6 4
      ♡ 8 6
      ◇ A J 7
      ♣ J 4 2

(j)   ♠ A 8 3 2
      ♡ 8 6 3
      ◇ A 10 4
      ♣ A Q 6

2) With each of these hands you bid a Stayman 2♣ after your partner's 1NT opening bid. How do you continue after the following rebids:

(i) 2◇?   (ii) 2♡?   (iii) 2♠?

(a)   ♠ K 10 6 5
      ♡ 7 5
      ◇ A Q 8
      ♣ Q 8 6 4

(b)   ♠ K 10 6 5
      ♡ 7 5
      ◇ A Q 8
      ♣ A 8 6 4

3) This time you have opened 1NT and responded 2♡ in answer to partner's 2♣ enquiry. What do you call after the following rebids:

(i) 2NT?   (ii) 3♡?

(a)   ♠ A 7 4
      ♡ K Q 9 6
      ◇ Q 10 4
      ♣ K 8 5

(b)   ♠ A J 7 4
      ♡ K 8 5 3
      ◇ 10 6 5
      ♣ A 9

(c)   ♠ A J 7 4
      ♡ K Q 5 3
      ◇ 10 6 5
      ♣ A 9

3. Responder's Rebid

Opener's Rebid is a Limit Bid

No bidding system can hope to spell out in detail what to do in every eventuality. The beauty and simplicity of Acol is that usually by the time opener has made his rebid, somebody has made a limit bid. If his partner understands the principles of good bidding he should then be able to use common sense to decide upon a sensible contract. The examples given below are far from comprehensive but they illustrate the thinking processes that should guide responder in the right direction after opener makes a limit rebid. He asks himself the following questions.

[1] Is the right level likely to be game or part-score? This will depend on whether the partnership could still have a combined total of 26 points.

[2] Is the right denomination no-trumps or a suit contract? If there is an 8-card major fit that should normally be preferred to no-trumps. If the only 8-card fit is a minor and game values are present it is usual to prefer 3NT unless there is an obvious weak suit, because making 9 tricks is far easier than struggling to fulfil an 11-trick contract.

Consider responder's second bid with the hands below after each of the bidding sequences given.

(i)	WEST	EAST	(ii)	WEST	EAST	(iii)	WEST	EAST
	1♡	1♠		1♡	1♠		1♡	1♠
	2♡	?		2♠	?		2NT	?

(a)	♠ A Q 6 3 2	(b)	♠ K J 6 3 2	(c)	♠ K J 6 3 2
	♡ K 7 2		♡ Q 7 2		♡ K 8
	◇ K 8		◇ K 8		◇ A Q 6 4
	♣ J 10 6		♣ Q 10 6		♣ 9 3

With (a) responder is confident game is worth bidding.

After (i) he knows the partnership has at least 8 hearts, so he concludes the auction with 4♡ [S].

After (ii) there is an excellent spade fit, so 4♠ [S] is obvious.

After (iii) East is still in doubt. Opener might still have 3 spades, in which case 4♠ will be best. If opener has 5 hearts then game in hearts should be bid. Otherwise 3NT should be sensible. On this hand we might advise beginners to settle for 3NT, as avoiding confusion is of vital importance, but in an improvers' book it is worth considering the meanings of the bids available to East.

East can repeat his own suit, 3♠ [S], as a sign-off. He would do this with a very weak hand and 6 spades. Holding a stronger hand with 6 spades he would jump to 4♠ [S]. At the moment there doesn't seem to be a way of showing 5 spades, but we will return to this later.

East can support West's suit. What would 3♡ mean? Here a general principle guides us. *You shouldn't need to sign off at the 3 level in a 7-card fit.* East cannot have a weak hand with 4 hearts, otherwise he would have bid 2♡ on the last round. This leads us to conclude that 3♡ should be forcing, showing 3-card support. Not only will that guide East/West to 4♡ if there is an 8-card heart fit, but if West has 4 hearts and 3 spades he can continue with 3♠ over 3♡, enabling 4♠ to be reached. East should bid 3♡.

Note that if opener's suit had been a minor suit it would be quite possible that on the first round of bidding responder concealed 4-card support in order to investigate a spade fit, so there seems to be a case for the sequence 1♢ 1♠ 2NT 3♢ to show a sign-off. Still, most experts prefer to forego this use, instead treating 3♢ as forcing.

With (b) responder is not certain of game opposite a minimum opening bid, so after (i) and (ii) he wants to pass the decision back to opener.

After (i) he raises to 3♡ [I].

After (ii) he raises to 3♠ [I].

After (iii) he knows opener is not minimum, so it is logical to bid 3♡ [GF], just like hand (a).

With (c) responder again wants to be in game.

After (i) he is far from sure of the denomination. He keeps the bidding alive with 3♦ [F]. It is a general principle that *in an uncontested auction a new suit at the 3-level is forcing*. Responder is prepared for any third bid by opener, intending to raise 3♠ (3-card support) to 4♠ [S], 3♥ (6-card heart suit) to 4♥ [S], or pass 3NT which should deny 3 spades or 6 strong hearts and show at least one stopper in clubs, the unbid suit.

After (ii) responder jumps to 4♠ [S].

After (iii) he tries 3♦ [F]. Again, a new suit at the 3-level in an uncontested auction is forcing. Opener will bid 3♠ [F] with 3 spades, repeat hearts with a strong suit, raise diamonds with excellent support or try 3NT if he has a club stopper. Note that this solves the problem of finding a 5–3 spade fit. Responder cannot bid a forcing 3♠ after a 2NT rebid, but he can bid a new suit and wait to see if opener can offer *delayed support*. Many experts would be prepared to bid 3♦ here with only 3 diamonds, just to see if opener can support spades. Actually it isn't dangerous. We said earlier that opener would require excellent support to raise diamonds. He is hardly likely to have this bearing in mind his failure to rebid 2♦. We think you must decide for yourself whether to try such manoeuvres. It would be foolish for us to advise you to take action that might make your partner unhappy.

Finally, we look at some sequences after a 1NT rebid. In the auctions below do you think the last bid is forcing?

(iv)	WEST	EAST	(v)	WEST	EAST	(vi)	WEST	EAST
	1♥	1♠		1♥	1♠		1♥	1♠
	1NT	3♦		1NT	3♥		1NT	3♠

In (iv) 3♦ is forcing, a new suit at the 3-level.

In (v) 3♥ is forcing with 3-card heart support.

In (vi) 3♠ is invitational, showing 6 spades. A rebid of your own suit after no-trumps, even with a jump, isn't forcing. West will pass only with a misfitting minimum.

Opener's Rebid is a Third Suit

The rebid of a third suit by opener is wide-ranging, showing 12–18 points. This often leaves responder with little idea of the final destination.

On the one hand he should be aware that his partner might be pretty strong, hence he will be reluctant to pass with 8 or 9 points (although sometimes that is unavoidable).

On the other hand it is more likely that opener does not have a great deal to spare, if only because there are far more hands in the range 12–15 points than 16–19. Responder might have made a forcing change of suit on the first round with a meagre 6 or 7 points, but it is his duty now to terminate the bidding quickly if he is weak. Below are four weak hands, each testing responder after the given auction.

WEST	EAST			
1◇	1♠	(d)	♠ K J 7 3	(e) ♠ K J 7 4 3
2♣	?		♡ Q 4 2	♡ 8 4
			◇ 10 6	◇ 9 7 3
			♣ Q 10 6 3	♣ Q 10 7
		(f)	♠ K J 7 3 2	(g) ♠ K Q 10 9 4 3
			♡ Q J 8 4	♡ J 4
			◇ J 7	◇ J 7
			♣ 9 3	♣ 9 3 2

With (d) he passes. What if opener has 18 points and game is missed? Tough luck!

With (e) he has no hope of game, but it would be wrong to pass 2♣. If your partner has bid two suits he is likely to either have greater length in the first or equal length. Therefore you should only leave him in his second suit if you have substantially greater length in that suit. If you are not strong enough to make two constructive bids (responder needs at least ten points for that) it is often correct to give *simple preference* to partner's first suit even if you are not too keen on it. Unlike most sequences where a player chooses to bid when he is free to pass, this guarantees no additional values. East should correct to 2◇.

Preference to 2◇ is also correct with (f). It is highly likely that West has 5 diamonds, so that won't be a stupid contract. If you don't like that, try looking at the alternatives! The spades are nothing like good enough for 2♠, 2NT would show 10–12 points and you will learn that 2♡ is not available as a natural bid.

With (g) East can bid 2♠, showing a weak hand with good spades. Opener will pass if he has a minimum opening bid with a singleton spade. The principle is summarised as follows:
With a weak misfitting hand, be delighted if you can find a sensible contract. Don't push the bidding higher in the vain hope that you will find a perfect contract.

We now repeat the bidding sequence and give 4 hands of 'intermediate' strength. With 10–12 points there are several rebids available to responder which are encouraging, but not forcing.

WEST	EAST	(h)	♠ K J 7 3	(j)	♠ K J 7 4 3
1◇	1♠		♡ 8 4 2		♡ 8 4
2♣	?		◇ 10 6		◇ A 7 3
			♣ A Q 6 3		♣ Q 10 7
		(k)	♠ K J 7 3 2	(l)	♠ K Q 10 9 4 3
			♡ A J 8 4		♡ A 4
			◇ J 7		◇ J 7
			♣ 9 3		♣ 10 3 2

With (h) East raises to 3♣ [NF] [L], showing 4-card support and 10–12 points.

With (j) East gives jump preference to 3◇ [NF] [L]. Unlike simple preference, jump preference guarantees 3-card support. If responder has at least 10 high-card points there is inevitably a sensible way of describing his assets on the second round of bidding without giving jump preference on doubleton support.

With (k) responder bids 2NT [NF] [L]. This shows a stopper in the unbid suit (hearts) and 10–12 HCP, unlike a direct response of 2NT which shows 11–12 HCP.

With (l) responder jumps to 3♠ [NF] [L] showing a strong 6-card suit and 10–12 points.

The Fourth Suit

We start by repeating the bidding sequence from the previous section, but this time we consider a hand that seems to leave East without a satisfactory continuation.

WEST	EAST	(m)	♠ A 10 8 4 3
1◇	1♠		♡ 9 7 3
2♣	?		◇ K 2
			♣ A 10 5

East is strong enough for an encouraging bid, but lacks the fourth club necessary for 3♣, the third diamond for 3◇ jump preference, the heart stopper for 2NT or the quality of spades required for 3♠.

Three suits have been bid and the answer is to bid the fourth suit, 2♡ [C] [F]. By now it is most unlikely that hearts is the correct denomination, so 2♡ is given a conventional meaning. Many players use it to show a 'half-stopper' in hearts, ♡ Q x or ♡ J x x. This has some logic in so far as while neither holding guards the suit by itself, both together provide a sure stopper. However, this use is very restrictive and leaves hands like (m) unbiddable.

Better is to play that the fourth suit simply shows at least intermediate values (10+ points), denies a suitable natural bid, and asks opener to make the most natural continuation. There are many different ideas on whether opener's reply to the fourth suit is forcing, but the following is easy to remember and practical.

The fourth suit at the 3-level is game-forcing.

The fourth suit at the 2-level is forcing for one round. If opener makes a minimum bid in any of the suits already bid naturally, or bids 2NT, responder can pass. If responder bids on after one of these minimum bids the auction becomes game-forcing.

Opener might have any of the following hands:

(n) ♠ 6 5 2
♥ 4
♦ A Q 7 6 3
♣ K Q J 4

(p) ♠ 5
♥ 4 2
♦ A Q 7 6 4 3
♣ K Q 6 4

(q) ♠ 5
♥ A Q 2
♦ A 8 7 6 3
♣ K 4 3 2

(r) ♠ K J 2
♥ 4
♦ A Q 7 6 3
♣ K Q 6 4

(s) ♠ 5
♥ 4 2
♦ A Q 7 6 3
♣ K Q 7 6 4

(t) ♠ 5
♥ A Q 2
♦ A Q 7 6 3
♣ K 4 3 2

(u) ♠ 5
♥ 8 6 4
♦ A Q J 6 5
♣ K Q 6 4

(v) ♠ K 5
♥ 8 6
♦ A K 9 6 5
♣ K 8 6 4

(w) ♠ K 5
♥ 8 6
♦ A K 9 6 5
♣ K Q 6 4

With (n) he rebids 2♠ [NF], showing delayed spade support.

With (p) he rebids 3♦ [NF], suggesting a 6-card suit.

With (q) he rebids 2NT [NF] showing at least one heart guard. By now he shouldn't be worried that his hand isn't balanced. There doesn't seem to be a fit, and the priority is to find a playable contract.

With (r) he rebids 3♠ [GF], showing 3-card support.

With (s) he rebids 3♣ [NF], suggesting 5–5 shape.

With (t) he rebids 3NT [GF].

With (u) he is rather stuck. 3♦ [NF] is the least of evils.

With (v) he rebids 2♠ [NF]. He would like a third spade for this bid, but must improvise. 2♠ often shows a good doubleton, because with 3-card spade support and a minimum opening West might have preferred a rebid of 2♠ to 2♣.

With (w) he bids 3♥ [C]. A raise of the fourth suit is also artificial and game-forcing, passing the buck back.

Finally, if responder has a hand suitable for jump preference or a jump rebid in his own suit, but too strong for these non-forcing bids he can create a forcing sequence by bidding the fourth suit and then making his chosen bid.

24

1) Your partner opens 1♡ and rebids 2♣ over your 1♠ response. How do you continue with these hands?

(a) ♠ J 8 6 4 3
♡ 7 3 2
◇ A Q 2
♣ 7 3

(b) ♠ J 8 6 4 3
♡ 7 3
◇ A Q 4 2
♣ 7 3

(c) ♠ J 8 6 4 3
♡ 7
◇ A Q 4 2
♣ 7 3 2

(d) ♠ J 8 6 4 3
♡ A 3 2
◇ A 6 2
♣ Q 7

(e) ♠ J 8 6 4 3
♡ A 3
◇ A Q 4 2
♣ 7 3

(f) ♠ K Q J 8 7 4
♡ 8 2
◇ 7 6 2
♣ 7 3

(g) ♠ K 8 6 5 3
♡ 7 5
◇ A J 9
♣ K 7 2

(h) ♠ K Q 6 5 3
♡ J 5 2
◇ 7 5
♣ Q 7 3

(j) ♠ K Q 6 5 3
♡ J 5
◇ 7 5 2
♣ K Q 2

2) What is your continuation as West with these hands after each of the following sequences?

(i)
WEST	EAST
1♡	2♣
2◇	2♠
?	

(ii)
WEST	EAST
1♡	1♠
2◇	3♣
?	

(a) ♠ K Q 5
♡ K J 7 6 2
◇ A Q 7 5
♣ 5

(b) ♠ 5
♡ K J 7 6 2
◇ A Q 7 5
♣ K Q 5

(c) ♠ 5
♡ A Q 7 6 2
◇ A Q 7 5 2
♣ 8 5

4. The Reverse

In the next few chapters we will investigate the principle that with a hand of minimum value, you should attempt to develop the bidding as cheaply as possible. Sometimes this has unexpected consequences. Consider these starts to the auction. In each case West clearly has both red suits.

(a) WEST   EAST   (b) WEST   EAST
     1♡   1♠   1◇   1♠
     2◇   2♡

In (a) he starts by bidding hearts, the higher of the two suits. When he makes his 2◇ rebid East can, if weak, pass 2◇ or give simple preference to 2♡. The option is available to play in either red suit at the 2-level.

In (b) East starts with diamonds, the cheaper suit. By the time he has completed his heart rebid the partnership can still legally play in 2♡, but 2◇ is no longer available. If responder wants to exercise that most common of cheap options, giving simple preference, he is forced to the 3-level. Paradoxically, the cheaper choice of opening bid results in a less economical rebid. This is why with touching 5-card suits it is right to start with the higher.

Of course sometimes it is correct to start with the lower and rebid the higher, but it should come as no surprise to you that for such an unnatural order there are strict requirements, concerning both the strength and shape of the hand. It is clearly absurd that if opener has 13 points and responder only 6, giving the opponents the majority of the HCP, the bidding should end up at the 3-level on what might be a none too impressive fit.

If you bid two suits in an order that forces partner to the three level if he wishes to give simple preference, you are *reversing*. A reverse by opener guarantees at least 5 cards in his first suit and 16 HCP, (occasionally 15 if opener has exceptional shape or a fit with responder's suit).

(c)	WEST	EAST	(d)	WEST	EAST	(e)	WEST	EAST
	1♦	1♠		1♦	2♣		1♥	2♦
	2♥	(3♦)		2♥	(3♦)		3♣	(3♥)

In each case West's rebid is a reverse and East's 3-level simple preference bid is shown in brackets.

If, as with sequences (c) and (d), the reversing bid occurs when West starts with the lower ranking suit and rebids the higher ranking at the 2-level (called a *low reverse*), he guarantees more cards in the first suit than the second (i.e., 5–4, 6–5 or 6–4 shape).

If, as with (e), the reverse involves West starting with the higher ranking suit and rebidding the lower suit at the 3-level without a jump (called a *high reverse*), the first suit may be longer or his shape may be 5–5 or 6–6.

A reverse after a response at the one-level is forcing only for one round. Therefore if responder has 9 or more points he must avoid a minimum second bid which can be passed. A second bid by responder (such as 2NT), which would show additional values after a non-reversing rebid by opener, indicates a minimum response after opener's reverse.

A reverse after a response at the 2-level is game-forcing because the combined values of an opener's reverse and responder's change of suit at the 2-level should be sufficient for game. Therefore responder can take his time and keep the bidding low even if he has a strong hand. *A sensible guideline is that if opener and responder have both shown extra values, then a game-forcing auction exists.* Responder's change of suit at the 2-level shows extra values. Consider opener's rebid in these auctions.

(f)	WEST	EAST	(g)	WEST	EAST	(h)	WEST	EAST	(j)	WEST	EAST
	1♥	2♦		1♥	2♦		1♥	2♦		1♥	2♦
	2♠			3♥			4♦			2NT	

If (f) opener has shown extra values by reversing. In (g) and (h) the jump rebids show at least 16 points. All three auctions are game-forcing, though traditional Acol would have considered (g) (a rebid in West's own suit) or (h) (West supporting East's suit) non-forcing.

You might wonder whether auction (j) should be forcing. Admittedly West's 15–16 opposite responder's 8+ doesn't seem quite enough to guarantee game, but you will see later that it isn't good tactics to change suit at the 2-level with a bare 8 points unless the hands seem to fit very well. Most Acol players wouldn't consider this auction to be forcing, but there are considerable advantages in playing 2NT as 15–19 HCP, game-forcing. In particular, it avoids opener having to jump to 3NT with 17–19 HCP, taking the auction too high to investigate sensibly the best denomination. Many experts raise the requirements to respond at the 2-level to 9 to 10 points, and play 2NT as game-forcing, but don't try it on your partner without warning! If you agree to play Acol partner will reasonably expect no-trump rebids to be limit bids, and that means a 2NT rebid as 15–16, not forcing.

Perhaps you feel that this little diversion is not really relevant. You might well be right, however the logic behind it is crucial to your understanding of bidding principles. A bidding system is a coherent whole, the status of a bid, forcing or otherwise, being determined by logic. If you choose to make stricter requirements for a 2-level change of suit there are consequences, in particular there is no need for a non-forcing 2NT rebid.

Opener's Jump Shift

♠ 4	♠ K Q J 5	WEST	EAST
♡ A K 8 7 4	♡ 6 3	1♡	1♠
◇ A Q J 5 3	◇ 10 7 2	3◇	3NT
♣ A J	♣ K 9 8 3		

West's jump rebid of 3◇ shows 19–20 points and is game-forcing. Replace his ♡K by the ♡J and he would rebid only 2◇. If opener's hand is too weak for a game-forcing jump-shift he must make a simple non-forcing rebid. He doesn't reverse just to show extra strength. To reverse you need extra strength *and* the right shape.

28

Quiz 3

1) In which of these unopposed sequences is opener reversing?
   Justify your answer by giving responder's preference bid.
   Also state whether opener's rebid is not forcing, forcing for
   one round, or game-forcing.

(i) 1◇ 1♠   (ii) 1♣ 1♠   (iii) 1♡ 2♣
     2♣   2♡   2◇

(iv) 1♡ 2♣   (v)   1♠ 2♡   (vi) 1♡ 2♣
     2♠   3◇   3◇

2) Give your opening bid with each of these hands. Also state
   your planned rebid over a 1♠ response.

(a) ♠ 9 5   (b) ♠ 9 5   (c) ♠ 9 5
    ♡ A 7 6 3   ♡ A K 6 3   ♡ A K 6 3
    ◇ A K J 7 5   ◇ A K J 7 5   ◇ A K J 7 5
    ♣ J 2   ♣ J 2   ♣ A 2

(d) ♠ 9 5   (e) ♠ 9 5   (f) ♠ 9 5
    ♡ A K J 7 5   ♡ A K J 7 5   ♡ A K J 7 5
    ◇ A 7 6 3   ◇ A K 6 3   ◇ A K 6 3
    ♣ J 2   ♣ J 2   ♣ A 2

3) Your partner opens 1◇ and rebids 2♡ over your 1♠
   response. What do you call with these hands?

(a) ♠ J 7 5 4 3   (b) ♠ J 7 5 4 3   (c) ♠ K Q J 7 6 4
    ♡ 7 6   ♡ 7 6   ♡ 7 6
    ◇ 7 3   ◇ K 3   ◇ 7 3
    ♣ A J 9 4   ♣ A J 9 4   ♣ 8 6 4

(d) ♠ K Q J 8 6 4   (e) ♠ A 7 5 4 3   (f) ♠ A 7 5 4 3
    ♡ 7 6   ♡ 7 6   ♡ A 7 6
    ◇ K 3   ◇ Q 8 5   ◇ Q 8 5
    ♣ 8 6 4   ♣ 8 6 4   ♣ 8 6

5.   Opener's Strategy

In chapter 1 we advised you that as opener you should classify your hand as balanced or unbalanced, and if balanced you should either open no-trumps, or open with a suit bid and rebid no-trumps over partner's change of suit. Of course that means that if you have a balanced hand in the range 12–14 HCP you *must* open 1NT because all no-trump rebids promise at least 15 HCP.

This means that sometimes you must open 1NT with a small doubleton. We won't pretend this is perfect, indeed you may find some partners object. However, all bidding theory involves weighing up the pros and cons of alternative actions and picking the one that turns out best in the long run. Later in this chapter you will see the great advantages in a bidding system where bidding two suits guarantees an unbalanced hand. In the meantime we suggest that opening 1NT with an unguarded suit is not as dangerous as you might expect for the following reasons.

(1)   Often your weakness and shortage will be opposite partner's strength and length.
(2)   If you do play in no-trumps with a weak suit after an uninformative auction the opposition don't always find the killing lead. The time to be really afraid of a weak suit is when you have told them what to lead by bidding the other three suits, or they have bid your weak suit.
(3)   Opening 1NT with a weak suit doesn't necessarily mean that you play in no-trumps. Partner has a wide variety of methods of investigating alternative contracts, including the admirable Stayman convention. It is well worth your referring back to hand (d) on page 15. West's 1NT opening bid should not prevent the correct contract of 4♠ being reached.

Opener has a Stronger Balanced Hand

Consider the hand shown below.

♠ K 9 5 2	♠ A 6 4 3	WEST	EAST
♡ K J 5 3	♡ Q 7 2	1♡	1♠
♢ A 4	♢ 9 5 2	3♠	4♠
♣ K Q 7	♣ A 10 8		

West has a balanced hand too strong to open 1NT. He opens 1♡, the *lower* of two *touching* 4-card suits. He is relying on East to introduce the spade suit if he has four spades. West had a 2NT rebid planned if East had responded 2♣ or 2♢. The reason that he opens the lower suit is that he doesn't intend to bid the other one, unlike the touching 5-card suits when you intend to show both and hence open with the higher one.

If opener has a major suit and a minor suit in a 4–4–3–2 hand too strong to open 1NT we suggest you open the major and rebid no-trumps at an appropriate level, forgetting the minor unless responder bids that suit.

Opening an Unbalanced Hand without a 5-card Suit (4–4–4–1 shape)
When opener chooses to introduce two suits rather than bid no-trumps on the first or second round of bidding he will usually have five cards in his first suit. The main exception is the 4–4–4–1 shape hand.

The best strategy for 4–4–4–1 shape hands is based upon the desired objective that an opening bid in a major suit followed by a rebid at the two level in a new suit should show at least five cards in the first suit.

With a singleton club open 1♡ and rebid 2♢ over 2♣.

With a singleton diamond open 1♣ and rebid 1♡ over 1♢.

With a singleton heart open 1♢ and rebid 1♠ over 1♡.

With a singleton spade open 1♢ and rebid 2♣ over 1♠.

To summarise, *with a red suit singleton open with the suit below the singleton. With a black suit singleton open the middle of the three touching suits.*

If you follow these rules the following inferences can be drawn by responder as soon as he hears opener start with a major suit.

An opening bid of 1♠ followed by a rebid in ♡, ♢, or ♣ *guarantees* five spades. Moreover an opening bid of 1♠ shows either a 5-card suit or a hand too strong to open 1NT, and hence intending a no-trump rebid. If opener has only four spades he will not have four hearts. You will see in the next chapter that responder can treat a 1♠ opener as a 5-card major and freely raise to 2♠ [L] on 3-card support.

An opening bid of 1♡ followed by a rebid in ♢ or ♣ guarantees five hearts with one exception. The sequence:

    1♡   2♣
    2♢

can contain only four hearts, but only on the rare occasions that opener has 4–4–4–1 shape with a singleton club.

False Preference by Responder

In the hand below West has plenty to spare for his 2♢ [NF] rebid, but he isn't strong enough for 3♢ [GF].

♠ 4	♠ K Q J 5	WEST	EAST
♡ A J 8 7 4	♡ 6 3	1♡	1♠
♢ A Q J 5	♢ 10 7 2	2♢	2♡
♣ A J 5	♣ K 9 8 3	2NT	3NT

East, knowing that West's rebid could conceal 18 points, does not want to pass and risk missing game. Armed with the knowledge that West has at least five hearts, he can give *false preference* to 2♡. A 5–2 fit will usually play better than a 4–3 fit. West is strong enough to make another game try and shows his club guard by bidding 2NT. East is then happy to forget the heart suit and settle for 3NT.

If a player gives preference to his partner's first suit and the partnership bids on, they should keep an open mind about the final denomination.

Opening a Hand with One 5-card Suit

If opener's hand shape is 5–4–2–2 or 5–4–3–1 he opens the 5-card suit. It is desirable to rebid the 4-card suit, but if he has less than 16 points he cannot reverse and may have to rebid his first suit.

(a)   ♠ K J 5 3   (b)   ♠ K J 5 3   (c)   ♠ K J 5 3
        ♡ K 6   ♡ K 6   ♡ K 6
        ◇ A Q 8 6 4   ◇ A Q 8 6 4   ◇ A Q 8 6 4
        ♣ 8 6   ♣ A 6   ♣ A Q

With each of these hands opener starts with 1◇.

With (a) he intends to rebid 1♠ [NF] over 1♡ but accepts that lack of reversing values compels a rebid of 2◇ [L] over a 2♣ response.

With (b) he can happily rebid 1♠ over 1♡ (not quite strong enough for a jump to 2♠ [GF]) or reverse into 2♠ [GF] over 2♣.

With (c) he will jump-shift to 2♠ [GF] over 1♡ or reverse into 2♠ [GF] over 2♣.

If the hand shape is 5–3–3–2 you have the choice of treating it as balanced or unbalanced. If your 5-card suit is a major you should bid it and rebid it unless you have available a convenient no-trump rebid or perhaps good 3-card support for partner's response. If your 5-card suit is a minor you should aim for a no-trump bid as early as possible unless the suit is exceptionally strong.

Opening a Hand with Two 5-card Suits

Unless you have the two black suits it is always correct to open the higher suit.

If the suits are touching it will be possible to rebid the other suit over any response.

If they are not touching you will always be able to rebid the second suit if you have sufficient values to reverse. If you have less than 16 HCP you mustn't reverse so if the response is inconveniently high you may have to rebid your first suit.

(d)   ♠ A Q 6 5 2   (e)   ♠ A Q 6 5 2   (f)   ♠ A Q 6 5 2
     ♡ 8 6   ♡ K 6   ♡ A Q
     ◇ A Q 9 7 5   ◇ A Q J 7 5   ◇ A Q J 7 5
     ♣ 6   ♣ 6   ♣ 6

With each of these hands you should open 1♠.

With (d) you will rebid 2◇ [NF] over a 2♣ response but you do not have the strength to reverse into 3◇ over a 2♡ response. Therefore you are forced to rebid 2♠ [L] over 2♡.

With (e) you will rebid 2◇ [NF] over 2♣ or reverse into 3◇ [GF] over 2♡. Note that in traditional Acol a third suit without a reverse can be passed, but many experts prefer to play it as forcing for one round if the response was at the 2-level. It is somewhat unsatisfactory to rebid a non-forcing 2◇ over 2♣ here when game is extremely probable.

With (f) you will jump to 3◇ [GF] over 2♣ or reverse into 3◇ [GF] over 2♡.

If your two suits are clubs and spades it tends to be right to open 1♣ with a guaranteed 1♠ rebid over a red suit response.

Quiz 4

1)   As dealer what do you bid with these hands? If you decide to open with a suit bid what is your rebid over partner's minimum response in each other suit?

(a)   ♠ A J 6 5   (b)   ♠ A K 6 5   (c)   ♠ A K 6 5
     ♡ K Q 8 3   ♡ K Q 8 3   ♡ K Q 8 3
     ◇ 8 5 2   ◇ 8 5 2   ◇ 8 5 2
     ♣ K 7   ♣ A 7   ♣ A K

(d)   ♠ 8 5   (e)   ♠ K 5   (f)   ♠ A Q
     ♡ K Q 7 5   ♡ Q J 7 5   ♡ K Q 7 5
     ◇ A 7 5   ◇ A 7 5   ◇ K 7 5
     ♣ K Q 8 5   ♣ K Q 8 5   ♣ K Q 8 5

2) As dealer, what do you bid with these hands? What is your rebid if partner makes a minimum response in your singleton suit?

(a)   ♠ K J 7 5   (b)   ♠ 4   (c)   ♠ A K 6 4
      ♡ A Q 8 2   ♡ A K 6 4   ♡ K J 7 5
      ♢ A K 6 4   ♢ A Q 8 2   ♢ 4
      ♣ 4   ♣ K J 7 5   ♣ A Q 8 2

3) In which of these unopposed sequences does opener guarantee five cards in his first suit?

(i)   1♠ 2♣   (ii)   1♠ 2♣   (iii)   1♠ 2♣
    2♢   2♡   2NT

(iv)   1♡ 1♠   (v)   1♡ 2♣   (vi)   1♡ 2♣
     2♢   2♢   2♠

4) With each of these hands state your opening bid and your rebid if partner responds in either of your short suits.

(a)   ♠ 8 5   (b)   ♠ J 5   (c)   ♠ K 5
      ♡ A 8 6 4 3   ♡ A K 8 4 3   ♡ A K 8 4 3
      ♢ A 7   ♢ A 7   ♢ A 7
      ♣ K Q 9 3   ♣ K Q 9 3   ♣ K Q 9 3

(d)   ♠ K J 6   (e)   ♠ K J 6   (f)   ♠ K J 6
      ♡ 7   ♡ 7   ♡ 7
      ♢ A J 8 7   ♢ A Q 8 7   ♢ A Q 8 7
      ♣ A 8 6 5 3   ♣ A K 6 5 3   ♣ A K Q 5 3

(g)   ♠ 7   (h)   ♠ 7   (j)   ♠ 7
      ♡ Q 9 8 4 3   ♡ A Q 8 4 3   ♡ A Q 8 4 3
      ♢ A 6   ♢ A 6   ♢ A Q
      ♣ A Q 8 5 4   ♣ A Q 8 5 4   ♣ A Q 8 5 4

6. Responder's Decisions

Responder Raises Opener's Major Suit

We saw earlier that if opener starts with a major suit he has either a 5-card suit or a balanced hand too strong to open 1NT (except for one 4–4–4–1 shape hand). This enables responder to freely raise 1♠ to 2♠ on 3-card support and he should prefer this course of action to a 1NT response unless his hand shape is exactly 4–3–3–3. If opener has five spades this will prove the better denomination. If opener has a balanced hand with 17+ points he will rebid no-trumps and it will be possible to escape from the 4–3 fit. Only if opener has a balanced hand with 15–16 points will he pass and then the 4–3 fit at the two level with ruffing value in the short hand should prove acceptable.

Consider the following hand:

♠ K Q 6 5	♠ J 7 4	WEST	EAST
♡ K 7 4	♡ A 8	1♠	2♠
◇ A Q 5 3	◇ K 9 6 2	2NT	3NT
♣ A 9	♣ 10 8 3 2		

The single raise of a major initially risks a 7-card fit but the correct rebid by opener suggests an alternative denomination. If East had four spades he would revert to a spade contract at the appropriate level.

Note that if opener chooses a 3♠ game try, or 3♣/◇/♡, a *trial bid* suggesting a second suit to help responder to judge how well the hands fit, he shows at least 5 spades.

Responder can also raise 1♡ to 2♡ with 3-card support, accepting the slight risk that opener has 4–4–4–1 shape with a singleton club. If he has four spades he prefers a 1♠ response, otherwise a 4–4 fit may be lost.

♠ A 10 8 7	♠ Q 9 6 5	WEST	EAST
♡ K 7 5 2	♡ A Q 9	1♡	1♠
◇ K 9	◇ 5 2	3♠	4♠
♣ A K 5	♣ 8 6 4 2		

West correctly opens the lower of touching 4-card suits, intending a no-trump rebid unless East responds 1♠. If East had incorrectly raised 1♡ to 2♡ the auction would have continued: 2NT 3NT.

While it is often correct to raise partner's major suit opening to the two level with only three cards in support, it is rarely correct to raise a minor suit or to give any jump raise without at least 4-card support.

Responder Changes Suit at the One Level

If responder can bid a 4-card major at the one level his priority is to bid this suit rather than respond 1NT or change suit at the two level. If he chooses to bid a 5-card minor suit at the two level it will be because he intends to bid his major suit on the second round (a responder's reverse). For this he requires the values that would enable him to bid 2NT, namely at least ten HCP.

(a)	♠ A Q 6 5	(b)	♠ A Q 6 5
	♡ J 7		♡ J 7
	◇ 6 4		◇ 6 4
	♣ Q 7 6 5 2		♣ A 7 6 5 2

Suppose opener starts with 1♡. With (a) responder must bid 1♠ because he is not strong enough to bid 2♣ and then reverse into 2♠ over 2♡. If he holds hand (b) he can reasonably reverse and should therefore bid his hand naturally, starting with his longest suit. Responder must decide whether he is strong enough to volunteer two bids before he chooses his first bid.

With two 4-card suits biddable at the one level responder should start with the lower, allowing opener to introduce the other if he has it.

With a 5-card suit and a 4-card suit, both biddable at the one level, responder normally bids his longer suit.

With two 5-card suits biddable at the one level responder starts with the higher, allowing him to introduce the lower suit without reversing if opener rebids no-trump.

Responder Jumps to 2NT or 3NT

Any immediate no-trump response denies a 4-card major biddable at the one level. Also a space-consuming leap to 3NT should be avoided unless your shape is exactly 4–3–3–3. Otherwise opener has no way of deciding what to do with 5–4–3–1 or 5–4–2–2 shapes. Suppose your partner opens 1♡ and you hold these hands:

(c)	♠ K 7 3 2	(d)	♠ A 10 5	(e)	♠ A 10 3
	♡ Q 6		♡ Q 6		♡ Q 6 4
	◇ A 8 7 6		◇ A 8 7 6		◇ A 8 7 6
	♣ A 10 5		♣ K 7 3 2		♣ K 7 3

With (c) a 1♠ response is correct. 3NT may well be the best contract but you can bid it next time. Even if partner raises 1♠ to 2♠ (which may contain only 3-card support) your next bid should be 3NT.

With (d) you should respond 2♣ and bid 3NT on your second turn. If you immediately leap to 3NT opener will remove to 4♡, if he has a 5-card suit. Replace the ♡Q by the ♡7 and a 2NT response would be reasonable, leaving room for opener to investigate a possible 5–3 heart fit below 3NT.

With (e) a 3NT response describes your assets perfectly.

Responder Changes Suit at the Two Level

A response at the two level shows one of the following:
1) 8+ high card points and a good enough fit with opener's suit to feel that if he rebids it you will be in a sensible contract (preferably Q x or better).
2) A hand strong enough to make another constructive bid. (Either a responder's reverse or 2NT require at least ten HCP.)

Note that there are many eight or nine point hands that are unsuitable for a response at the two level. Admittedly opener will have his rebid planned over any response, but why force him to rebid a poor quality 5-card suit and then pass when you know that might leave him in a 5–1 fit? It is a golden rule of bridge that *when you have more than one possible bid with a poor hand, pick the bid that keeps the bidding low.* This is the same principle that defines a reverse. A player should not force his partner to make an unnecessarily high bid unless he has good reason to believe that a higher level contract will be successful.

Consider your response to a 1♡ opening with each of the following hands.

(f)	♠ 6 5 4	(g)	♠ K 5 4	(h)	♠ 5 4
	♡ 5		♡ 5		♡ K 5
	♢ K 6 5 3		♢ K 6 5 3		♢ 8 6 5 3
	♣ A J 9 4 3		♣ A J 9 4 3		♣ A J 9 4 3

With (f) your reply will be 1NT, allowing partner to pass if he has a minimum opening bid.

Your fit for partner's heart suit is no better with (g), but this time you are strong enough continue with 2NT over a 2♡ rebid, therefore you can respond 2♣.

Hand (h) is only worth one bid, but this time you are not alarmed at the prospect of a 2♡ rebid, therefore respond 2♣.

The 1NT Response

Usually a no-trump bid early in the auction promises no singleton or void. The 1NT response is the exception to this. Because of the requirements of other responses, particularly the change of suit at the two level, the 1NT response becomes the dustbin bid. Every hand that is too strong to pass but doesn't fit into any other response is catered for by 1NT. On rare occasions it could even conceal a singleton in an unbid suit!

Over an opening bid of 1♢, 1♡ or 1♠ a 1NT bid simply says 'I have 6–9 points and I can't think of anything better to bid.' The logic is simple. If you change suit at the two level you force partner to find a rebid but by using up a lot of space you limit his options. While he will always have a rebid available he may not be over-enthusiastic about it. If you respond 1NT he doesn't have to rebid.

Of course it is possible to keep the traditional meaning of 1NT over 1♣ (8–10 points and 3–3–3–4 shape), because with 6–7 points you can raise 1♣ to 2♣. Sadly you cannot insist on this luxury over a 1◇ opening. Try to find a response to a 1◇ opening with a weak 3–3–1–6 hand unless you can bid 1NT!

The higher the denomination of the opening bid, the more likely it is that a 1NT response is unbalanced. Opener should realise that if he opens 1♠ and hears a 1NT response his partner won't have 3-card support unless his shape is exactly 4–3–3–3 and he may even be void. Therefore opener must not repeat a 5-card suit.

It is, of course, perfectly sensible to sign off in a 5-card club suit if partner responds 1NT to your 1♣ opening bid because you know he has at least 3-card support.

Quiz 5

1) Your partner, as dealer, opens 1♡. How do you respond with these hands?

(a) ♠ K 8 6 4
♡ A 8 5
◇ 8 6
♣ 9 8 6 2

(b) ♠ 8 6
♡ A 8 5
◇ K 8 6 4
♣ 9 8 6 2

(c) ♠ J 5 3
♡ A 8 5
◇ K 8 6 4
♣ 9 8 6

2) Partner raises your 1♡ opening to 2♡. How do you rebid with these hands?

(a) ♠ K 8 6 4
♡ A 9 5 3
◇ K J 5
♣ A 4

(b) ♠ K 8 6 4
♡ A K J 3
◇ K J 5
♣ A 4

(c) ♠ A K 7
♡ K 9 5 3 2
◇ A J 5
♣ A 4

3) You raise opener's 1♡ to 2♡. His rebid is 2NT. How do you continue with these hands?

(a) ♠ 8 6 4
♡ J 9 7 6
◇ A 5
♣ 9 7 5 2

(b) ♠ 8 6
♡ Q 9 7
◇ A 6 5 3
♣ 9 8 7 5

(c) ♠ 8 6
♡ J 9 7
◇ A 6 5 3
♣ K 8 7 5

4) Your partner, as dealer, opens 1♡. How do you respond with these hands?

(a) ♠ A 6 4
♡ 6
◇ A 10 9 6 2
♣ 7 5 3 2

(b) ♠ A 6 4
♡ 6
◇ A 10 9 6 2
♣ K 5 3 2

(c) ♠ Q 7 6 4
♡ 6
◇ 9 7 6
♣ A K 5 3 2

(d) ♠ Q 7 6 4
♡ 6
◇ K 7 6
♣ A K 9 5 4

(e) ♠ Q 7 6 4
♡ 7 6 5
◇ A Q 5
♣ A Q 5

(f) ♠ A Q 5
♡ 7 6 5
◇ Q 7 6 4
♣ A Q 5

(g) ♠ A Q 5
♡ 7 6
◇ Q 7 6 4
♣ A Q 6 3

(h) ♠ A Q 5
♡ 7 6 5
◇ Q 7 6 4
♣ A 6 3

(j) ♠ A Q 5
♡ 7 6
◇ Q 7 6 4
♣ A 8 6 3

5) How do you respond to a 1♣ opening bid with these hands?

(a) ♠ K Q 6 4
♡ K 6 5 3
◇ 8 6 2
♣ 7 5

(b) ♠ K 7 6 5 3
♡ K 7 6 4 2
◇ 8
♣ 7 5

(c) ♠ K 6 5 3
♡ 7 5
◇ 8 6 2
♣ K Q 6 4

7. Developing your Judgement

The theme of this chapter is that although you seemingly have a rigid method of evaluating your hand through the 4–3–2–1 point count, not all points are equally valuable.

Good and Bad points

In this book we assume that you play the weak no-trump, showing 12–14 HCP. That doesn't mean that you have to open all hands that superficially contain 12 points. Consider these 3 hands.

(a)	♠ 8 6 3 2	(b)	♠ 8 7 4 2	(c)	♠ K Q 10 2
	♡ K Q		♡ Q 6 3		♡ 8 5 3
	♢ K Q J		♢ A K Q		♢ A J 10
	♣ J 8 3 2		♣ J 8 2		♣ Q 10 9

A 1NT opening with (a) would invite a substantial penalty. Honour cards without supporting small cards are clearly not worth their point count. The ♡ K Q will only provide one trick whichever defender has the ♡A. If you had ♡ K Q x then you would score two heart tricks if your right hand opponent (RHO) had the ♡A. Equally ♢ K Q J is unlikely to be worth more than two tricks. Even if partner has the ♢A, unless he had four or more diamonds the duplication of values will reduce the trick-taking capacity. The only thing that would revive your enthusiasm would be if partner shows interest in the red suits. *Points in partner's suits are especially welcome.*

In general you should subtract a point for holdings like K Q doubleton, K Q J tripleton, or singleton honours unless partner has bid the suit. That makes (a) worth just 10 points, nowhere near an opening bid.

(b) Doesn't have these holdings, but it has a number of other unattractive features.

Firstly, the high cards are in the short holdings. *Prefer a hand with the high cards in the long holdings.* Replace the ♠2 by the ♢2 and the ♢ A K Q might promote the ♢2 into a trick. There are no honour cards to help promote the ♠2.

Secondly, there are no tens and nines which so often become promoted to extra tricks. ♣ J 8 2 opposite the ♣ A 4 3 is most unlikely to furnish a second club winner, while ♣ J 10 9 opposite the same holding would be highly likely to be worth two club tricks.

Thirdly, isolated honours like ♡ Q 6 3 and ♣ J 8 2 are often a disappointment. Imagine the two holdings below:

(d)   ♡ Q 6 3   (e)   ♡ K Q 3
   opposite   opposite
          ♡ K 5 2   ♡ 6 5 2

With (d) you are unlikely to make more than one heart trick. With (e) you can make two heart tricks if West has the ♡A. *Honours supporting each other in the same hand enhance each others' value. Isolated honours are less effective.*

Only hand (c), which is better than many supposedly 13 point hands, is worthy of an opening 1NT.

In Acol it is acceptable to open the bidding third-in-hand with lighter than normal values, but you should be strongly influenced by whether the bid you are considering will help partner find the best opening lead if your side loses the auction.

(f) ♠ K Q   (g) ♠ 9 6   (h) ♠ K 6
    ♡ J 7 4 3 2   ♡ K Q 7 3 2   ♡ Q 9 7 3 2
    ◇ Q 6 4 3 2   ◇ A J 9 3 2   ◇ J 9 4 3 2
    ♣ K   ♣ 4   ♣ A

It would be misguided to open with (f) in any position. The only opening bid that would give you a rebid would be 1♡, and you hardly want to encourage partner to lead from a holding like ♡ K x. Pass this hand.

Hand (g) is well worth opening 1♡ in any position. Firstly, having your high cards in your long suits gives your hand greater playing strength, as they might help promote the low cards to winning status. Secondly, you would welcome a heart lead. Replace the $\diamond$J by the $\diamond$4 and you should still venture a third in hand 1$\heartsuit$.

Hand (h) has the same quota of high cards as (g), but with the high cards in short suits it is not worth opening.

Of course if the hand is stronger it may be necessary to open the bidding with high cards in the short suits, but you should be less inclined to bid aggressively in the uncontested auction, and more willing to double an enemy intervention. Consider the South hands below after this somewhat energetic start to the auction.

SOUTH	WEST	NORTH	EAST
1$\spadesuit$	2$\heartsuit$	4$\spadesuit$	5$\heartsuit$
?			

(j)	$\spadesuit$ A K 10 9 6 3	(k)	$\spadesuit$ J 10 9 6 5 3	(l)	$\spadesuit$ A J 9 6 5 3
	$\heartsuit$ 8 2		$\heartsuit$ A K		$\heartsuit$ K Q J
	$\diamond$ A J 8 5		$\diamond$ J 8 5 3		$\diamond$ J 8 5
	$\clubsuit$ 4		$\clubsuit$ A		$\clubsuit$ 4

With (j) you have excellent playing strength, and comparatively little defensive strength. It would not surprise you greatly to lead the $\clubsuit$A against 5$\heartsuit$ and see it ruffed, leaving you with just the $\diamond$A to contribute to the defence. Compete to 5$\spadesuit$.

The texture of hand (k) is entirely different. Firstly, you have three certain defensive tricks. Secondly, your prospects in 5$\spadesuit$ would be less attractive. You should double 5$\heartsuit$.

Of course the argument for doubling 5$\heartsuit$ with (l) is overwhelming. The bidding makes it certain that partner has a singleton or void heart, making your $\heartsuit$ K Q J worthless in a spade contract.

If you have secondary honour cards which are likely to be opposite partner's shortage, be inclined to defend rather than outbid your opponents.

The Delayed Game Raise

As a beginner you might have been told to raise 1♡ to 4♡ with 13–15 points, or fewer points if you have a good fit with wild distribution. You might raise 1♡ to 4♡ with (m) or (n) but with different motives.

(m)	♠ 2	(n)	♠ A J 9 4	(p)	♠ K Q 3
	♡ K 9 8 5 3		♡ K J 7 3		♡ A Q 9 6 5
	◇ Q J 10 6 2		◇ A 6 2		◇ 4
	♣ 7 3		♣ 7 3		♣ A J 4 2

With (m) you hope to make 4♡, but even if you don't you will not be surprised to find your opponents could have made 4♠. Your excellent fit in hearts makes it quite likely that each side can make a high-level contract, so you want to pre-empt the bidding quickly to a high level. However, you don't want partner to go hunting for a slam.

With (n) you expect to make 4♡ by sheer power and you don't fear competition. Rather than jump immediately to 4♡ you should make a *delayed game raise*. Firstly, make a forcing, waiting bid of 1♠. Then, whatever partner rebids, jump to 4♡. The message is: heart support, useful spades.

The spotlight then shifts to opener. Suppose he holds (p). This hand has only 16 HCP, but he should be most encouraged by the excellent fit. He has ♠ K Q 3 in responder's side suit, a singleton in one minor suit and the ace of the other. He would be fully justified in checking two aces are not missing via a Blackwood 4NT and settling for 6♡.

The moral here is that counting points should not become a mindless ritual. If you have a good fit with partner a slam may be possible with a relatively meagre total.

Before leaving (p), it is worth looking at opener's rebid. After a 1♠ response to his 1♡ opening bid he would like to show two features: his 4-card club suit and the encouraging spade support. He must content himself with 2♣ [NF], confident that if responder gave preference to 2♡ a 2♠ continuation shows his hand perfectly: 16 or so HCP, 3 spades, 5 hearts, 4 clubs and therefore a singleton diamond. Even if he wanted to support spades immediately he couldn't do so because he is too strong for 2♠ and lacks the 4-card support necessary for a jump to 3♠.

However suppose you replace the ♣A by the ♣10. This time if opener rebids 2♣ he is not strong enough to continue with 2♠ if responder gives preference to 2♡. Therefore he does best to show his 3-card spade support immediately.

The principle is to *consider whether your hand is worth a third bid before deciding on your second bid*.

Responder's Jump Shift

Modern theory is for responder to avoid jumping in a new suit on the first round just because he holds 16 points. With a balanced 16 points responder can make a series of forcing bids, allowing opener to show his hand. Responder needs a good suit to jump shift. The jump shift shows two main hand types. Responder would jump to 2♠ opposite a 1♡ opening bid with either of these hands.

(q)	♠ A Q J 10 5 3	(r)	♠ A Q 10 9 3
	♡ 9 4		♡ A J 7 2
	◇ A Q 2		◇ A 2
	♣ K 9		♣ 6 4

With (q) he would follow up with 3♠ to show a one-suited hand with truly excellent spades. With (r) he would bid hearts next time to show support for opener's suit and good spades (at least 5 cards in length). Such detailed information should enable opener to judge whether the hands fit well for a slam. In the sequence below responder can count 13 tricks: 5 spades (♠ A x x x x would not justify 2♠), 6 hearts and two minor suit aces.

♠ K J 5	♠ A Q 10 9 3	WEST	EAST
♡ K Q 10 6 3 2	♡ A J 7 4	1♡	2♠
◇ 9	◇ A 2	3♠	4♡
♣ A 10 2	♣ 6 4	4NT	5♠
		7♡	

Quiz 6

1) Which of these hands would be worth an opening bid as dealer with neither side vulnerable? Would your decision be different third in hand?

(a) ♠ A K J 4 2
♡ Q 10 9 7 4
◇ 9 4
♣ 2

(b) ♠ A K J 4 2
♡ 10 9 8 7 4
◇ 9 4
♣ 2

(c) ♠ 10 9 8 7 4
♡ A K J 4 2
◇ 9 4
♣ 2

(d) ♠ A Q 10 3
♡ J 10 8 2
◇ A 10
♣ J 9 7

(e) ♠ Q 8 4 2
♡ Q 6 4 3
◇ A K
♣ J 8 4

(f) ♠ A 9 5 2
♡ J 10 2
◇ 4
♣ K Q 9 8 3

2) Your partner responds to your 1♠ opening bid with 2♣ and opposite your 2◇ rebid he jumps to 4♠. How do you continue?

(a) ♠ A J 7 3 2
♡ A 9
◇ A 8 6 2
♣ Q 7

(b) ♠ A Q 7 3 2
♡ Q 8 7
◇ K Q J 7
♣ 2

(c) ♠ K Q J 3 2
♡ K Q 7
◇ K Q J 7
♣ 2

3) You raise your partner's 1♠ opening to 2♠, and he continues with a trial bid of 3◇, a game try in spades showing also a second suit. Do you bid 3♠ or 4♠?

(a) ♠ K 8 7
♡ 7 6 4 2
◇ K J 6 3
♣ 6 2

(b) ♠ K J 7 2
♡ Q 6 4
◇ 9 5 2
♣ Q 9 3

(c) ♠ K Q 7 2
♡ A 8 3
◇ 9 5 2
♣ 8 6 3

8. Competitive Decisions

This is a practical chapter. It is not meant to elaborate on the basic theory you will have picked up in a beginners' book, but rather to deal with the sort of awkward decisions you face at the table and see how your action depends on the bids both of your partner and your opponents. There is not a quiz at the end, but you might like to try to answer the numerous questions posed before you read the answers.

Double, Overcall, or Pass?

The books say that the ideal shape for a take-out double is 4–4–4–1 with a singleton in the opposition suit. Would that life were always so simple! What would you bid with the following hands at love all if your RHO opens 1♡?

<table>
<tr><td>(a)</td><td>♠ K J 3 2
♡ 9 4
♢ A J 6 3
♣ K 9 7</td><td>(b)</td><td>♠ K 9 7
♡ 9 4
♢ A J 6 3
♣ K J 3 2</td><td>(c)</td><td>♠ K J 3 2
♡ 6 4 3
♢ A Q
♣ A 8 7 3</td></tr>
<tr><td>(d)</td><td>♠ K J 7 3 2
♡ 8
♢ A Q 6 3
♣ K 7 2</td><td>(e)</td><td>♠ K 7 2
♡ 8
♢ A Q 6 3
♣ K J 7 3 2</td><td>(f)</td><td>♠ A 10 6 2
♡ A 2
♢ K J 6 4
♣ K J 8</td></tr>
</table>

The principle is that the more you are suited to hearing a response in any unbid major, or majors, the more you should be inclined to choose a double.

Double with (a). If your ♡4 were the ♣4 you could double with one fewer point.

With (b) we would advise a pass. Don't make a minimum double if your support for the unbid major is dubious.

Double is safer than you might think with (c). You will see that partner will respond 1♠ if at all possible, and if he bypasses all the intervening bids to respond 2♢ he is very likely to have a 5-card suit.

Overcall 1♠ with (d). If you double you won't uncover a 5–3

spade fit. Double followed by spades shows a strong hand, but there is no reason why you can't overcall 1♠ and double for takeout if an enemy 2♡ is passed back to you.

Double with (e). The quality of the club suit is rather unsatisfactory for a 2-level overcall. Losing a 5–3 club fit won't be the end of the world.

With 4 spades and a doubleton heart prefer double to 1NT with (f).

Although theoretically a take-out double asks partner to bid his best suit, usually the doubler will be looking for a major suit fit. In the following auctions East should try to ensure his spade support gets a mention.

SOUTH	WEST	NORTH	EAST
1◇	Dbl	No	?

(g) ♠ Q 5 3 2   (h) ♠ J 5 3 2   (j) ♠ Q 5 3 2
    ♡ 9 2   ♡ 9 2   ♡ 9 2
    ◇ A 10 5 4   ◇ 9 7   ◇ 9 7
    ♣ 9 7 4   ♣ J 9 7 3 2   ♣ A 9 7 3 2

With (g) he should prefer 1♠ to 1NT.

With (h) 1♠ is a more helpful reply than 2♣. He is worth only one bid and the major gets priority.

With (j) he might start with 2♣ because he is strong enough to volunteer a spade bid if he gets another chance.

The Problems facing Opener's Partner

Below are six hands. For each hand we will consider how opener's partner will respond after hearing opener call 1♣. We look at his actions, and his reasoning, in four cases:

(i)   The intervening hand passes.
(ii) The intervening hand overcalls 1♡.
(iii) The intervening hand overcalls 1NT.
(iv) The intervening hand makes a take-out double.

Frequently the decision will not be clear-cut. You will also see that his action is not only dependent on his hand. *It is strongly influenced by the intervention.*

(k) ♠ A Q 10 9 6   (l) ♠ K 8 3   (m) ♠ 8 5 4
     ♡ 8 5 3   ♡ 7 2   ♡ A Q 8 3
     ◇ 10 4   ◇ 10 9 4 3   ◇ Q 8 2
     ♣ K 6 5   ♣ K J 4 2   ♣ 7 6 3

(n) ♠ 10 4   (p) ♠ Q 8 3   (q) ♠ 9 7 2
     ♡ 9 6 4   ♡ K Q 10 9 3   ♡ 8 4 3
     ◇ A K 10 7 5 3   ◇ K 8 3   ◇ Q 9 8 2
     ♣ A 7   ♣ 9 4   ♣ A Q 4

(i) If the intervening hand passes the answers need little explanation.

(k) 1♠ [F1R]   (l) 2♣ [L]   (m) 1♡ [F1R]
(n) 1◇ [F1R]   (p) 1♡ [F1R]   (q) 1◇ [F1R]

(ii) Generally opener's partner will try to ignore the overcall and bid as in (i). However, there are two problems that might dictate a change. Firstly, the overcall may have taken away bidding space. Here a 1◇ response has been ruled out by the 1♡ overcall. Secondly, while it might have been reasonable to chance a no-trump response with a weak suit if the opponents hadn't bid, now you require a stopper in their suit. Therefore:

(k) 1♠ [F]. No change.
(l) 2♣ [L]. No change.
(m) 1NT [L]. Without the overcall you would have been duty-bound to show your 4-card major.
(n) 2◇ [F1R]. One level higher than you planned.
(p) Double. For penalties! This bid guarantees very good trumps, not just lots of HCP. A double of a suit bid is only for takeout if partner has not previously made a bid. (A pass does not count as a bid.)
(q) 2♣ [L] or pass. You cannot bid 1NT without a guard in their bid suit. You can either improvise with 3-card support or pass, content with the knowledge that partner has another chance. The overcall has freed you from the obligation to bid with a weak hand.

(iii) The guide-line is simple if the intervening hand overcalls 1NT. Double for penalties if you have 9 or more HCP (making it likely that your side has the majority). Failure to double therefore shows *less* than 9 HCP and common sense dictates that any other bid is not forcing. Therefore:

(k) Double. For penalties.
(l) 2♣ [L]. No change.
(m) Pass. Reluctantly.
(n) Double. Overcaller's partner must have a very weak hand and this will be their catastrophe.
(p) Double.   (q) Pass, or perhaps 2♣.

(iv) Generally it is wise to ignore the double, as after all it hasn't taken any bidding space away. The main change worth considering is that it pays to be aggressive in support of partner's suit, pre-empting before the opponents find a fit. The rule is that if you have 4-card or better support for partner you should bid one level higher than you would have done without the double. Therefore:

(k) 1♠ [F1R]. No change.
(l) 3♣ [L]. Pre-emptively one level higher than you would have bid without the double. Change the ♠K for the ♠7 and you would bid 2♣ [L] rather than pass.
(m) 1♡ [F1R], despite the fact that RHO probably has four hearts. 1NT is a reasonable alternative. You wouldn't bid a weak 4-card suit after a take-out double.
(n) 1◇ [F1R]. No reason not to bid naturally.
(p) 1♡ [F1R]. Ditto.
(q) Pass, 1NT [L] or 2♣ [L]. To bid this diamond suit with RHO probably holding four is not a pleasant thought.

The Problems facing Overcaller's or Doubler's Partner

Here are six hands. For each we will consider how East will call after the following sequences. Again you will see that East's action depends not only on his own hand but also on the circumstances. Sometimes he will seem to have no perfect bid available and must decide upon the best compromise. In general, common sense is the key.

(i)	SOUTH	WEST	NORTH	EAST	(ii)	SOUTH	WEST	NORTH	EAST
		1♠	No	?		1♡	1♠	No	?

(iii)	SOUTH	WEST	NORTH	EAST	(iv)	SOUTH	WEST	NORTH	EAST
	1♡	Dbl	No	?		1♡	Dbl	2♡	?

(r)	♠ J 8 7 3	(s)	♠ J 6 5 4	(t)	♠ K Q 3
	♡ 10 6 2		♡ Q 3		♡ 8 3
	◇ Q 7 6		◇ K 7 6 3		◇ A 6 3 2
	♣ 10 9 3		♣ A 9 4		♣ A J 7 5

(u)	♠ K J 9 3	(v)	♠ 2	(w)	♠ 2
	♡ 9 6 3 2		♡ A J 7 6		♡ 9 5 4 2
	◇ K J 8 3		◇ K 6 5 2		◇ A Q 10 9 8 3
	♣ 2		♣ Q J 7 2		♣ A 9

(i)   West has 12+ HCP and at least four spades. With 3-card support East can sometimes raise to 2♠, but never to 3♠ or 4♠. He can pass if he so chooses. Therefore:

(r)	Pass	(s)	3♠ [L]	(t)	2♣ [F1R]
(u)	3♠ [L]	(v)	2♣ [F1R]	(w)	2◇ [F1R]

(ii)   West has 9–16 HCP and at least five spades. 3-card support is always acceptable but slightly more HCP are required to bid game. Therefore:

(r)   Pass. Going nowhere opposite 9–16 HCP.

(s)   2♠ [L]. Hopeful of game opposite 14+ HCP.

(t)   4♠ [S]. A minimum raise to game with only 3-card support. Don't forget that West might have less than opening strength for his overcall.

(u)   4♠ [S]. Partly pre-emptive and partly hoping to make. Not many HCP but your hand has excellent shape and partner is probably very short in hearts.

(v)   1NT [L]. 9–12 HCP and at least one heart guard. You need more points to respond 1NT to an overcall than you would to respond 1NT to an opening bid because the overcall guarantees fewer points than the opening bid. 2NT [L] [NF] would show 13–14 HCP and 3NT 15+ HCP.

(w)   2◇ [NF]. A change of suit by overcaller's partner shows an excellent suit and dislike of the overcaller's suit. It is mildly constructive but not forcing. If East wanted to force West to bid again he would jump in his suit (3◇) or *cue bid* the enemy suit (2♡ [C]).

(iii)   West has 11+ HCP and has *demanded* that East remove the double, however weak. The only time that East could choose to pass is if he had an outstanding heart suit in an otherwise worthless hand (e.g., ♡ K Q J 10 8 6). Then he would be *positively choosing hearts as trumps*, not opting out of his responsibility to bid. West's most likely holding in the enemy suit is a singleton. Therefore:

(r)   1♠ [NF]. 0–7 HCP.

(s)   2♠ [L]. 8–12 HCP or slightly fewer with good shape.

(t)   2♡ [C] [GF]. A game-forcing cue bid to give the partners time to exchange information.

(u)   2♠ [L]. Same as (s).

(v)   2NT [L]. 11–12 HCP (1NT would show 6–10) and good heart guards. Don't worry about the spades. Partner has them for his double. 3♣ would be a reasonable alternative.

(w)   5◇ [NF]. Excellent playing strength.

(iv)   West has demanded that East take out the double, but because North has already taken it out, East is relieved of his obligation to bid with rubbish. If he chooses to bid it is called a *free bid* and should show about 6 points, just as though he had responded to an opening bid. Therefore:

(r)   Pass. Too weak for a free bid.

(s)   2♠ [L] or 3♣ [L]. A close decision. You will certainly bid to 3♠ if they continue with 3♡.

(t)   3♡ [C]. A game-forcing cue bid. If partner bids 3NT you will pass. Alternatively raise a suit bid to game.

(u)   3♠ [L]. Less HCP than (s) but more shape.

(v)   2NT [L], or perhaps a penalty double.

(w)   5◇. As with (iii) (w).

How High Should We Bid in Competition?

With the hand below at love all try to work out:

(i)   How many tricks North/South can make in 4♠.
(ii) How many tricks East/West can make in 4♡.

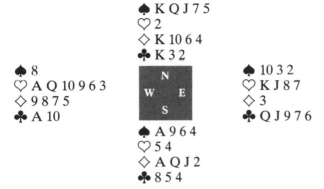

The answers to (i) and (ii) are both ten. The bidding might follow the following auction:

WEST	NORTH	EAST	SOUTH
1♡	1♠	4♡ (1)	4♠ (2)
5♡ (3)	No	No	Dbl (4)
No	No	No	

(1) A pre-emptive move based on a good fit.
(2) He might not have bid this freely but knowing both sides have a good fit it pays to be aggressive. He *doesn't* know whether 4♠ can be made, or indeed whether they can make 4♡, but it is quite likely that one of them can make so even if he is bidding an unmakeable contract (called *sacrificing*) it might turn out to be a bargain.
(3) West has two more hearts than he has shown with his opening 1♡, increasing his playing strength in hearts and also making it more likely that North/South can make 4♠. It won't be a disaster to turn +100 into −100. What *would* be serious is to concede −420 when +450 was possible.
(4) The bidding has to stop sometime, even with both sides having a 9- or 10-card fit. Such sequences where both sides have shape and fit often stop at the five level.

Below are three hands. For each of them consider East's action at love all after the following sequences:

(i)
SOUTH	WEST	NORTH	EAST
1♠	Dbl	2♠	?

(ii)
SOUTH	WEST	NORTH	EAST
1♠	Dbl	4♠	?

(iii)
SOUTH	WEST	NORTH	EAST
1♠	2♡	2♠	?

(iv)
SOUTH	WEST	NORTH	EAST
1♠	2♢	3♠	?

(x) ♠ 10 6 3
♡ A J 10 7 3
♢ 8 2
♣ 8 7 5

(y) ♠ A 4 3
♡ 4
♢ K 10 9 4 2
♣ 8 7 5 4

(z) ♠ A 8 4 3
♡ 9 7 6
♢ Q 5 3
♣ K 9 3

(x) (i) 3♡. You are likely to have a good heart fit.
(ii) Pass. A bit too shapeless for 5♡. (Don't forget, West might not have four hearts.) Even so 5♡ could be a winner!
(iii) 5♡ (or 4♡ if you are of a nervous disposition). You have at least a 10-card fit. Since the bidding is likely to end up high in the end, pre-empt violently and let them guess!
(iv) Pass. A poor hand with no great fit.

(y) (i) 3♢ or 4♢. A cross-ruff could provide lots of tricks.
(ii) 5♢. It sounds as if you have a good, and shapely, diamond fit and they have a similar spade fit.
(iii) Pass. You have a misfit with partner. That is *good for defending but bad for playing*.
(iv) 5♢. An outstanding 10-card fit. Let them guess.

(z) (i) Pass. Your side has most of the HCP but you have nothing worth mentioning.
(ii) Double. But you are not *totally* confident.
(iii) 3♡. Very shapeless but just about worth a raise.
(iv) Pass. Not confident of making 10 tricks.

9. More Competitive Bidding Theory

Overcalling an Enemy 1NT

An opening bid of 1NT has two important merits. Firstly, it uses up bidding space, making it harder for opponents to overcall. Secondly, it gives precise information to your partner, so that if an opponent misjudges an overcall partner is well placed to make a penalty double. If RHO opens 1NT and you have a good 6-card suit it is safe to overcall, but balanced and two-suited hands pose problems.

The most important difference against 1NT is that double is for penalties, not take-out. It is right to double a weak 1NT on almost any hand with 16 or more HCP. Consider these hands if your RHO opens 1NT.

(a)	♠ A K 8	(b)	♠ Q 10 7	(c)	♠ A Q J 7 6 3
	♡ K 9 6		♡ A K 8		♡ 10 7 2
	◇ A 8 7		◇ A J 8 7		◇ 9 6
	♣ 9 7 4 3		♣ K 9 2		♣ K 10

(d)	♠ A Q J 7 6 3	(e)	♠ Q 9 7 6 4	(f)	♠ A 2
	♡ A 8		♡ K J 9 7 3		♡ 4 3
	◇ K 9		◇ 7		◇ 7 4 3
	♣ K 6 2		♣ A 9		♣ A K Q J 9 8

With (a) pass. Just because you would have opened 1NT doesn't mean you should bid now.

With (b) double. This is risky but correct. If opponents have the majority of HCP they might make 1NT doubled, but if your side has the majority of HCP (more likely as you have more than the opener) you should pick up a healthy penalty. You have done your bit. It is now down to the two unknown hands, opener's partner and your partner.

With (c) bid 2♠, showing a good suit but fewer than 16 HCP.

With (d) double. You are too strong for an overcall.

With (e) pass. If you feel frustrated, thinking that partner

56

probably has a fit for one of your suits, you may well be right. As you gain experience you will learn that there are plenty of conventional bids available over a 1NT opening bid to show a two-suited hand.

With (f) double. You can double with fewer than 16 HCP if you have the necessary playing strength to beat 1NT.

What Happens after 1NT is Doubled?

When 1NT has been doubled for penalties one or other side may be in serious trouble. If opener's partner is very weak he *knows* he is in trouble because his partner has defined his hand very closely with the 1NT opening (12–14 HCP and balanced). If the doubler's partner is very weak he *fears* he might be in trouble, but he doesn't know because his partner could have well over 20 HCP. Below are three hands. Consider your action, as East, with each hand after both of the following auctions at love all:

(i)	SOUTH	WEST	NORTH	EAST		(ii)	SOUTH	WEST	NORTH	EAST
	1NT	Dbl		?			1NT	Dbl	No	?

(g) ♠ 9 7 3 2   (h) ♠ Q J 5 4 3   (j) ♠ K Q J 9 8 4 3
    ♡ J 8 4 3   ♡ 8 4   ♡ 2
    ♢ 8 6 2   ♢ 8 5 4   ♢ K J 8
    ♣ J 6   ♣ K Q J   ♣ 6 4

(g)   (i)   Pass, and hope for the best. Incidentally, after the double 2♣ would be natural, not Stayman.
        (ii) Pass. You have nowhere to go! In any case partner may have enough to beat 1NT on his own.

(h)   (i)   2♠. It is usually right to sign off in a 5-card suit. Even though your side has most of the HCP you may still fail if North has a strong suit to cash.
        (ii) Pass. Firstly, you should beat 1NT doubled easily and secondly, unlike opener's partner, you have no guarantee that your partner is balanced. If you try to play in spades you may find a low singleton spade in dummy.

(j)   (i)   4♠. As (h) though this time you are worth game.

56

(ii)   4♠. You should make this even if partner has no spades at all and the penalty for beating 1NT doubled may be insufficient as partner can hardly be expected to lead a spade.

Bidding after 1NT is doubled is often difficult. Since even the experts sometimes disagree you shouldn't worry too much if your borderline decisions go wrong.

Continuations after a Take-out Double

Consider these West hands after the following auction.

SOUTH	WEST	NORTH	EAST
1♣	Dbl	No	1♠
No	?		

(k)	♠ A J 9 5	(l)	♠ A J 9 5	(m)	♠ A J 9 5
	♡ K 7 6 2		♡ K 7 6 2		♡ A K 7 2
	◇ K J 8 7		◇ A Q J 4		◇ A Q J 4
	♣ 8		♣ 8		♣ 8

Should you bid further, hoping that game is possible, or should you pass, taking the view that since South has opening values game is unlikely? There is a good, simple rule of thumb available. Imagine this mythical auction:

SOUTH	WEST	NORTH	EAST
	1 other suit	No	1♠
No	?		

Decide the level to which you would have supported spades and then bid one less to allow for the fact that partner may have no HCP at all. Therefore:

With (k) Pass. In your mythical auction you would have raised to 2♠, but then partner would have at least 6 HCP.

With (l) raise to 2♠, instead of 3♠.

With (m) raise to 3♠, instead of 4♠.

Doubling for Take-out without Support for all the Other Suits

How should you bid these hands if RHO opens 1♣?

(n) ♠ A J 10 9 4   (p) ♠ A K J 9 4 2   (q) ♠ A K 5
      ♡ A 9   ♡ 8 7   ♡ A K 7
      ◇ A Q 6   ◇ A 4   ◇ 10 7 3
      ♣ A 10 2   ♣ A K 7   ♣ K Q J 8

They all have one thing in common. They are *too strong* for a simple overcall. If they were a little weaker you would have a comfortable bid available.

Hand (n) is too strong for 1♠ (9–16 HCP) and lacks the 6-card suit necessary for a jump overcall of 2♠.

Hand (p) is too strong for a jump overcall of 2♠.

Hand (q) is too strong for a 1NT overcall (16–18 HCP).

The solution in each case is to start with a double and on the next round to make the bid for which you were too strong. Partner will initially think you have a 3-suited hand but when you ignore this choice of suit the message will be clear. He should notice a double that asks him to choose and then ignores his choice! Therefore:

With (n) Double and then bid spades as cheaply as possible.

With (p) Double, and then jump in spades.

With (q) Double and then bid 1NT [L] (19–20 HCP).

Note that if you ask partner to choose and then ignore his choice you are showing a strong hand, not a hand where you had hoped for another response. If you make a take-out double with less than 16 HCP *you must pass partner's minimum reply*.

Protective Bidding

So far we have examined your defensive bidding after your RHO opens the bidding. Suppose now that LHO's opening bid is followed by two passes, so that if you pass the auction is over. You cannot be as choosy as your partner who may have had to pass with 15 HCP, otherwise you may miss game.

Below are three hands. Consider how you would handle them after the following auction:

SOUTH	WEST	NORTH	EAST
1♣	Pass	Pass	?

(r) ♠ J 10 8 6 3
♡ 7 2
◇ A 6 4
♣ Q 8 5

(s) ♠ J 9 7 4
♡ A 7 3 2
◇ A 7 5 3
♣ 5

(t) ♠ 7 6 2
♡ A 5 2
◇ A J 8 6
♣ Q 7 5

As West you would have passed any of them without a second thought. However, bidding now is less risky than it seems. Consider the implications of the auction so far.

South: 1♣. 11–20 HCP.

West: Pass. Could have anything up to 15 HCP.

North: Pass. Pitifully weak. At most 5 HCP.

What does this add up to? Your opponents have at most 25 HCP, probably a lot less. *Your partner must have some HCP* and he could have quite a good hand, yet has been unable to find a bid. Probably the HCP are evenly divided between the two sides and each side can make a part-score in its chosen suit. You must therefore contest the part-score rather than lie down and let the opposition play in their chosen suit at the one level. Your hand is called the *protective hand* and you need roughly three fewer HCP to bid. Therefore:

With (r) overcall 1♠. In the protective position you needn't worry about suit quality.

With (s) double, for take-out.

With (t) bid 1NT, showing 11–14 HCP. The lower end of the protective 1NT overcall is a full five points lower than an immediate 1NT overcall.

Of course after protective action by East, West must exercise discipline. East is effectively bidding 3 of West's points for him. Don't forget, East may know for certain that West has these points. West should mentally subtract 3 points from his assets before deciding on a response.

Generally speaking, if your opponents have found a fit and are about to pass the hand out at a low level you should try to compete. Consider the auction below.

SOUTH	WEST	NORTH	EAST	♠ J 7 4 3 2
1◇	No	2◇	No	♡ K 8
No	?			◇ 9 3 2
				♣ A 8 5

With such a poor quality suit you rightly chose not to overcall 1◇ with 1♠, but it is right to try 2♠ now.

Firstly, your partner will be aware that you didn't overcall first time, and will suspect your suit is poor.

Secondly, you know he has some points, otherwise why are your opponents passing the hand out in 2◇? He will not feel inclined to bid on because he will know you are bidding some of his high cards for him.

Thirdly, they clearly have a fit, which increases the probability that you also have a fit.

The Redouble

If your opponents double your partner's suit opening you often ignore the double (unless you intend to raise your partner's suit), but it would be foolish not to take advantage of the new option open to you, the redouble.

(i)	SOUTH	WEST	NORTH	(ii)	SOUTH	WEST	NORTH
	1♡	Dbl	Redbl		1♡	Dbl	2NT

In (i) it would be pointless to redouble with a heart fit, because that is precisely when they will remove it. Instead redouble with (u). The message is that you have at least 10 HCP, and a *misfit* with partner. The misfit makes taking a penalty double more attractive than declaring.

(u)	♠ K J 10 5	(v)	♠ A Q 10 2	(w)	♠ A Q 9 7 3
	♡ 7		♡ 7 6		♡ A 7
	◇ K J 9 3		◇ K 9		◇ 8 4 3
	♣ Q 10 9 5		♣ Q 10 7 6 3		♣ 9 5 2

If they pass out 1♡ redoubled you expect partner will make it by brute force. If they escape into their own suit you will make a penalty double. The message to partner is that the hand belongs to your side, and that the opponents should not be allowed to play in any contract undoubled.

You can redouble with (v) also. If they alight in 1♠ or 2♣ then you intend to double. If they bid 2♢ you will be happy if partner can double, otherwise you will try 2NT.

It would be pointless to redouble with (w). Of course you want to double spades, but that is wishful thinking. Inevitably they will have a minor-suit fit, and if they jump the bidding you will find it difficult to investigate a spade fit. Prefer to respond 1♠. Redouble suggests that you can double at least two of their suits.

Since responder will normally redouble with a hand that would have been worth a 2NT response, the 2NT response in auction (ii) seems irrelevant. Since it is normal to bid one level higher after a double with a fit with partner, use 2NT conventionally to show a genuine raise to 3♡.

Bidding the Enemy Suit

What do you think it means if RHO opens 1♡ and you bid 2♡, or your RHO overcalls partner's opening 1♢ with 1♡ and you bid 2♡? You are most unlikely to want to play in hearts, since even if you do have an 8-card fit with your partner the missing hearts are undoubtedly breaking badly. A bid of the opponent's suit is called a *cue bid* and is conventional and forcing to game. Suppose RHO opens 1♡ and you hold these hands:

(x)　♠ K Q J 8 3　　(y)　♠ A K Q J 9 8 2
　　　♡ A　　　　　　　　♡ −
　　　♢ A K Q J 6 2　　　♢ A Q 10
　　　♣ 9　　　　　　　　♣ A Q J

In each case overcall 2♡ to buy yourself time.
With (x) you will show your diamonds and spades and let partner choose between 4♠, 5♢, 6♢ or 6♠.
With (y) you will show a powerhouse with spades.

Quiz 7

1) Below are nine hands. Consider your bidding plan if your RHO opens 1♦. If you start with a double how do you intend to continue after partner has taken it out?

(a) ♠ A 7
     ♡ K J 8 4
     ♢ Q 10 3
     ♣ A 6 5 2

(b) ♠ A 7
     ♡ K Q 8 4
     ♢ K J 3
     ♣ A 6 5 2

(c) ♠ A K Q 10
     ♡ K 8 6 4
     ♢ 7
     ♣ K 8 5 2

(d) ♠ A Q 3
     ♡ A 10 8
     ♢ Q J 9 3
     ♣ A Q J

(e) ♠ Q 9 7
     ♡ A K J 7 6 5
     ♢ 7
     ♣ A Q 10

(f) ♠ A Q 10 9 7
     ♡ A 6
     ♢ 7 5
     ♣ A K 7 4

(g) ♠ A K 3
     ♡ A J 3
     ♢ Q J 9 2
     ♣ A Q J

(h) ♠ K Q 6
     ♡ A K J 7 6 5
     ♢ 7
     ♣ A Q 10

(j) ♠ 7
     ♡ A 7 5
     ♢ A K J 9 7
     ♣ K J 7 2

2) For the four sequences below decide how you would bid with the three East hands shown.

(i)
SOUTH	WEST	NORTH	EAST
1NT	2♡	No	?

(ii)
SOUTH	WEST	NORTH	EAST
1NT	2♣	No	?

(iii)
SOUTH	WEST	NORTH	EAST
1NT	Dbl	No	?

(iv)
SOUTH	WEST	NORTH	EAST
1NT	Dbl		?

(a) ♠ Q 6 5 3 2
     ♡ 8 2
     ♢ 9 6 2
     ♣ 10 5 4

(b) ♠ Q J 10 9 8
     ♡ 9 6 4 3
     ♢ J 10 9 3
     ♣ –

(c) ♠ Q 6 5 3 2
     ♡ K 7 2
     ♢ K J 4
     ♣ 6 2

3) For each of the sequences below decide how you would bid with the three East hands shown.

(i)	SOUTH	WEST	NORTH	EAST	(ii)	SOUTH	WEST	NORTH	EAST
		1♡	Dbl	?			1♡	1♠	?

(iii)	SOUTH	WEST	NORTH	EAST	(iv)	SOUTH	WEST	NORTH	EAST
		1♡	1NT	?			1♡	2♣	?

(v)	SOUTH	WEST	NORTH	EAST	(vi)	SOUTH	WEST	NORTH	EAST
		1♡	2♠	?		1♢	Dbl	No	?

(vii)	SOUTH	WEST	NORTH	EAST	(viii)	SOUTH	WEST	NORTH	EAST
	1♢	1♠	No	?				1♢	No
						No	Dbl	No	?

(ix)	SOUTH	WEST	NORTH	EAST	(x)	SOUTH	WEST	NORTH	EAST
			1♢	No				1♢	No
	No	1♠	No	?		No	1♠	2♣	?

(a)	♠ 6 4	(b)	♠ K J 8	(c)	♠ 5 4 2
	♡ K 8 4 3		♡ A 4		♡ K 6
	♢ K J 6 2		♢ J 7 4 3		♢ J 9 6
	♣ 8 6 2		♣ 8 6 4 3		♣ K Q 10 8 3

4) For the two sequences below decide how you would bid with the three West hands shown.

(i)	SOUTH	WEST	NORTH	EAST	(ii)	SOUTH	WEST	NORTH	EAST
	1♡	No	2♡	No		1♣	No	2♣	No
	No	?				No	?		

(a)	♠ K 8 4 3	(b)	♠ Q 5 4 3 2	(c)	♠ 9
	♡ 9 7		♡ 6 5		♡ K J 7 4
	♢ A J 6 4		♢ A J 6		♢ 7 5 3 2
	♣ 9 6 2		♣ 9 6 2		♣ A Q 9 5

10. Common Suit Combinations

In this chapter we consider common suit combinations that give you a choice between taking a finesse and playing out your top cards hoping the missing enemy honour falls (called 'playing for the drop').

Suppose you have bid to a contract of 4♠ and your contract depends on avoiding any spade loser from the trump suit shown below in (a). You start by cashing the ♠A, both defenders following low, and continue with the ♠2. West follows with another low spade. Should you play dummy's ♠J (successful if West has the ♠Q) or dummy's ♠K (necessary if East has the ♠Q)?

(a) ♠ K J 6 4   (b) ♡ K J 10 5

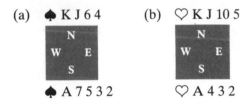

      ♠ A 7 5 3 2   ♡ A 4 3 2

Try looking at 'vacant spaces'. Assume you have no clue as to the defenders' distribution in other suits. We now know 3 of West's 13 original cards (including the opening lead), and only 2 of East's. West has 10 'vacant spaces', while East has 11. This suggests that East is marginally more likely to hold the ♠Q, suggesting that you should play dummy's ♠K.

Please be reassured at this stage. You don't need to calculate 'vacant spaces' every time you have to make a decision between taking a finesse and playing for the drop. It is widely known that holding 9 cards in a suit, missing just the queen, it is usually correct to play for the drop. However, the concept of vacant spaces shows it is a marginal decision, and almost any clue that might indicate otherwise should persuade you to take the finesse.

Maybe West opened 1NT (showing 12–14 points) and you are missing only 16 points. Maybe East opened with a pre-emptive 3♣, announcing great length in clubs and implying corresponding shortage in the other suits. In either of these cases you should finesse the ♠J.

The crucial point is that you should not be dogmatic. There is a well-known phrase: 'Eight ever, nine never'. This is an *aide-memoire* to help you remember that holding 9 cards in a suit missing the queen you usually shouldn't finesse (never) while with 8 cards the finesse is usually correct (ever). There are thousands of players who quote this phrase mindlessly, with the result that although it contains more than a grain of truth, it does more harm than good. Such substitutes for thinking have no uses for bright improvers.

In the absence of clues that might suggest otherwise the Australian expert and writer, Tim Bourke, has formulated a number of excellent *aide-memoires* which we use throughout this chapter.

If the number of cards outstanding in the suit is less than, or equal to, twice the number of higher honours you hold, play for the drop.

If the number of cards outstanding in the suit is greater than twice the number of higher honours you hold, take the finesse.

As seen by considering the spade suit in (a), the decision is borderline when the number of cards outstanding exactly equals twice the number of higher honours you hold.

Try applying this to the heart suit in (b). There are 5 outstanding hearts. You hold 2 higher honours than the missing queen. 5 is greater than twice 2, so finesse. Start by cashing the ♡A in case East has the ♡Q singleton. Then finesse North's ♡J.

Now consider the suits below, assuming ample entries to either hand. In each case you need to take as many tricks as possible in the suit.

66

(c) ◇ A K Q 10   (d) ◇ A K Q 10 3

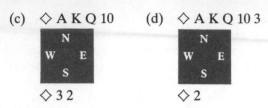

◇ 3 2   ◇ 2

You should finesse dummy's ◇10 in (c) and (d). You have 7 diamonds missing, and you have only 3 higher honours than the ◇J. 7 is greater than twice 3. With (c) you should cash the ◇A first just in case East has the ◇J singleton.

(e) ♣ A K Q 10   (f) ♣ A K Q 10 3 2

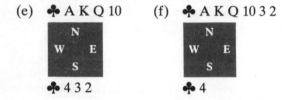

♣ 4 3 2   ♣ 4

You should play for the drop in (e) and (f). You have 6 clubs missing, and you have 3 higher honours than the ♣J. 6 equals twice 3. The decision here is close and you should be swayed by any clues to the contrary.

Analogous situations

How would you play the suits below to make maximum tricks?

(g) ♠ Q 10 6 4   (h) ♡ Q 10 9 5

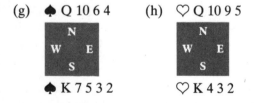

♠ K 7 5 3 2   ♡ K 4 3 2

Take (g) and upgrade the rank of all your significant high cards by one. You now have the spade suit already seen in (a)! The two suits are analogous, and they should be tackled in the same way. This time it is worth leading a low spade from dummy towards your ♠K (just in case East has the ♠A singleton). If the ♠K loses to West's ♠A you will lead the ♠2 towards dummy later. Then, if West follows low, play for the drop as you had 4 spades missing and 2 honours higher than the ♠J.

Equally you should play (h) like (b). Lead low to the ♡K and finesse the ♡10.

Common Variations

How would you play the suits below if you were hoping for 5 tricks? Again assume ample entries to either hand.

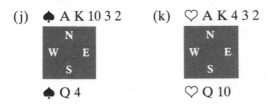

(j) ♠ A K 10 3 2   (k) ♡ A K 4 3 2

♠ Q 4   ♡ Q 10

There is no reason not to cash the ♠Q followed by the ♠A and ♠K in (j). You have 6 spades missing and 3 honours higher than the ♠J. You will make 5 tricks if the spades break 3–3 or if either defender has the missing ♠J doubleton.

Can you see the difference in (k)? This time if you play for the drop in hearts you are not in a position to benefit from the ♡J falling doubleton as your ♡10 will be engulfed by one of dummy's high cards. Playing for the drop only works if hearts break 3–3 which, as you will see in chapter 11, has significantly worse prospects of success than the simple heart finesse. The principles described earlier assume you can succeed on a bad break if the missing honour is in the hand with shortage. In this case you should use another suit to enter the North hand and finesse your ♡10.

Now consider how to handle the suits shown below, assuming ample entries to the North hand.

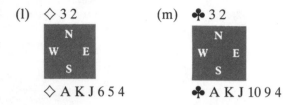

(l) ◇ 3 2   (m) ♣ 3 2

◇ A K J 6 5 4   ♣ A K J 10 9 4

You have just 5 cards missing including the queen so, in the absence of significant clues to the contrary, taking the finesse is undoubtedly correct. The question is whether or not you should first cash the ace in case West has the queen singleton.

In (l) there can be no possible reason not to cash the ◇A. If West does indeed have the ◇Q singleton you will lose a diamond trick, but a careless first round finesse of the ◇J would leave you with two diamond losers.

How about (m)? Cashing the ♣A will undoubtedly be beneficial if layout (n) applies, but how about layout (p)?

(n)   ♣ 3 2   (p) ♣ 3 2

♣ Q   ♣ 8 7 6 5   ♣ 5   ♣ Q 8 7 6

♣ A K J 10 9 4   ♣ A K J 10 9 4

Suppose you cash the ♣A, cross to dummy with another suit and finesse the ♣J. It will win, but West will show out. East still has ♣ Q 8, but you no longer have a club in dummy to repeat the finesse, resulting in a club loser.

You need common sense rather than advanced mathematics to resolve this. Cashing the ♣A is best if West has the ♣Q singleton. Taking two finesses is best if West's singleton is any of the missing low clubs, four times as likely.

Quiz 8

1) ♠ A Q J 10 9
   ♡ A K
   ◇ Q 8 6
   ♣ A K Q

   ♠ 8 7 6 5 4
   ♡ 6 4
   ◇ A K 2
   ♣ J 6 3

Contract: 7♠ *Lead:* ◇J
When you switch to the ♠4
West follows with the ♠2.

2) ♠ A Q J 10 9 8
   ♡ A K
   ◇ Q 8 6
   ♣ A K

   ♠ 7 6 5 4 3
   ♡ 6 4
   ◇ A K 2
   ♣ J 6 3

Contract: 7♠ *Lead:* ◇J
When you switch to the ♠3
West follows with the ♠2.

3) ♠ J 7 3 2
   ♡ J 5 4
   ◇ A 6
   ♣ 8 6 3 2

   ♠ A Q 6 5 4
   ♡ 6 3 2
   ◇ K Q
   ♣ A K Q

Contract: 4♠ *Lead:* ♡K
The defenders cash 3 heart
tricks and switch to the ◇J.

4) ♠ J 7 3 2
   ♡ J 5 4
   ◇ A 6
   ♣ 8 6 3 2

   ♠ A Q 10 5 4
   ♡ 6 3 2
   ◇ K Q
   ♣ A K Q

Contract: 4♠ *Lead:* ♡K
The defenders cash 3 heart
tricks and switch to the ◇J.

11.   Using the Percentages

In chapter 10 we mentioned briefly, without giving details, that a 3–3 break was less likely than a finesse. It is time now to consider more closely the role of percentages in bridge. Please don't feel the need to learn their figures, just try to understand the implications.

Number of cards missing in a suit	Approximate probability of the distribution of the enemy cards	
8	4–4 is 33%	5–3 is 47%
7	4–3 is 62%	5–2 is 31%
6	3–3 is 36%	4–2 is 48%
5	3–2 is 68%	4–1 is 28%
4	2–2 is 41%	3–1 is 50%
3	2–1 is 78%	3–0 is 22%
2	1–1 is 52%	2–0 is 48%

Some of these have an easy memory guide by simply reversing the numbers:

The 3–2 break occurs about ⅔ of the time.
The 4–1 break occurs about ¼ of the time.
The 4–2 break occurs about 2⁄4 of the time.

It helps to know that if you are missing an *even* number of cards (greater than two) in a suit a good break is less likely to yield you a trick than a finesse (50%), but if you are missing an odd number a good break is more likely to work than a finesse.

An easy way to remember the practical application is summarised as follows:

An *odd* number of missing cards will usually break *evenly*.
An *even* number of missing cards will usually break *oddly*.

Suppose you have two possible lines for your contract. One depends on a heart finesse, presumed to be 50% because you have no clues as to the position of the missing honour. The other depends on the clubs breaking favourably.

If you hold 8 clubs (missing 5, an *odd* number) the enemy clubs will break 3–2 68% of the time, far better than a finesse. If you have 7 clubs (missing 6, an *even* number) you will be favoured by a 3–3 break only 36% of the time.

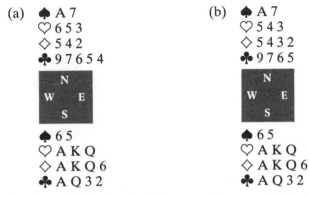

(a) ♠ A 7
 ♡ 6 5 3
 ◇ 5 4 2
 ♣ 9 7 6 5 4

N
W E
S

 ♠ 6 5
 ♡ A K Q
 ◇ A K Q 6
 ♣ A Q 3 2

Contract: 3NT *Lead:* ♠K

(b) ♠ A 7
 ♡ 5 4 3
 ◇ 5 4 3 2
 ♣ 9 7 6 5

N
W E
S

 ♠ 6 5
 ♡ A K Q
 ◇ A K Q 6
 ♣ A Q 3 2

Contract: 3NT *Lead:* ♠K

In each case you have 8 top tricks and need a ninth. Your last entry to dummy has been removed by the opening lead so that if you want to take a club finesse, now may be your last opportunity. If you do finesse the ♣Q and lose to the ♣K you will sink under a deluge of spades and will never be able to profit from a kind diamond break, should one exist.

With (a) the probability of a 3–3 diamond break is less than 50%, but with (b) a 3–2 diamond break will occur more often than 50%. Finesse the ♣Q with (a) and play on diamonds with (b).

It is most unsatisfactory that you have been forced to choose between your two options so soon. On a less threatening heart lead you could have tried cashing your ◇ A K Q to see if the suit was breaking, only subsequently falling back on the club finesse as a last resort.

More on Combining your Chances

Sometimes you have more than one chance of fulfilling your contract, and you can combine your options provided you try them in the right order. Consider these hands:

(c)   ♠ Q 7 6 4   (d)   ♠ A
      ♡ Q 7   ♡ K 10 9 8 2
      ♢ K J 9 8   ♢ 8 5
      ♣ 9 6 2   ♣ A K 5 4 2

      ♠ A K 2   ♠ 7 5 4
      ♡ 5 4   ♡ A Q J 7 6
      ♢ A Q 10 5 4   ♢ K 9 2
      ♣ A K J   ♣ 8 6

Contract: 5♢   Lead: ♡3 to   *Contract: 6♡   Lead: ♠Q*
East's ♡K. East cashes the
♡ A and switches to the ♣3.

Playing (c) you may well eventually have to take the club finesse for your eleventh trick, but that can wait. Rise with your ♣A, draw trumps and cash the ♠ A K Q. If spades have broken 3–3 the ♠7 is now a winner, allowing you to discard the ♣J. If not, you can finesse the ♣J. In fact the club finesse is your most promising option as a finesse (50%) is more likely than a 3–3 break (36%), but you can only combine your options by trying spades first.

    Similarly playing (d) your most promising line is a diamond finesse, however, it costs nothing to take the ♠A, draw trumps, cash the ♣ A K and ruff the ♣2. If clubs have broken 3–3 the ♣ 5 4 will allow you to discard two diamonds from your hand, rendering the diamond finesse unnecessary.

If you have a choice of plays for your contract, test first the line that does not lose the lead.

Quiz 9

1) ♠ 8 7
♡ Q J 10
♢ 8 7 4
♣ A Q J 7 6

♠ A 6
♡ A K 9
♢ A K J 10 9
♣ 10 9 8

Contract: 3NT *Lead:* ♠K

2) ♠ A Q 8 7
♡ A K J
♢ K 7
♣ K 7 6 4

♠ K J 10 9 6
♡ 10 9 7
♢ 6
♣ A Q J 3

Contract: 6♠ *Lead:* ♡2

3) ♠ 2
♡ A Q
♢ A K Q 7
♣ A K Q J 10 9

♠ A K 4 3
♡ 7 5 4 3
♢ 6 5 4
♣ 8 7

(i) *Contract:* 7NT *Lead:* ♢J
(ii) *Contract:* 7NT *Lead:* ♣6
(iii) *Contract:* 7NT *Lead:* ♡8
(iv) *Contract:* 7NT *Lead:* ♠Q

4) ♠ 2
♡ A Q
♢ A K Q 7
♣ A K Q J 10 9

♠ A K 4 3
♡ 7 5 4 3
♢ 6 5 4 2
♣ 8

(i) *Contract:* 7NT *Lead:* ♢J
(ii) *Contract:* 7NT *Lead:* ♣6
(iii) *Contract:* 7NT *Lead:* ♡8
(iv) *Contract:* 7NT *Lead:* ♠Q

12. Safety Plays

Consider your campaign of play for the hand below for each of the given contracts.

```
        ♠ 8 2
        ♡ 9 6
        ◇ 10 2
        ♣ A K Q 7 4 3 2
              N
          W        E
              S
        ♠ A K 6 4
        ♡ A 7 4
        ◇ A K 6 5
        ♣ 6 5
```

(i)   *Contract:* 6NT   *Lead:* ♠J
(ii)   *Contract:* 3NT   *Lead:* ♠J
(iii) *Contract:* 3NT   *Lead:* ♡J

For (i) you can give yourself a pat on the back for reaching an excellent slam with just 27 HCP. You have 12 easy tricks, barring the unlikely event of clubs breaking 4–0.

In (ii) your first reaction is likely to be one of disappointment that you have missed 6NT, but that is no reason to fail in 3NT! Of course you have 12 tricks if clubs break 3–1 or 2–2, but about 10% of the time they will be 4–0, and then unless you are careful you will be held to 8 tricks. Suppose you start by winning the ♠A and taking the ♣A, East discarding a heart. You can continue with the ♣K, ♣Q and ♣2, driving out the ♣J, but you then have no further entry to dummy to reach your three established club winners. The way of ensuring your contract irrespective of the location of the missing cards, is to duck a club (i.e., play a low club from each hand) at trick 2. Most of the time you will simply score one fewer overtrick, but that is of little consequence when compared to the value of your game contract. This is called a *Safety Play* and is rather like an insurance policy. You pay a relatively small premium and usually gain nothing in return. But when disaster strikes, your policy saves you from a loss that would really hurt.

In (iii) the safety play is inappropriate for a different reason. Of course you can afford the 'overtrick' premium, but the trouble this time is that greater danger lurks. The opening lead has knocked out your only heart guard (even if you withheld your ♡A until trick 3), and if you give them a club trick it is all too likely that ungrateful opponents will take enough heart tricks to sink your contract.

You should cultivate the habit of looking for a safety play to ensure your contract when the contract seems easy. A practical approach is to ask yourself what can go wrong, and see if you can safeguard against that eventuality. Consider the hands below.

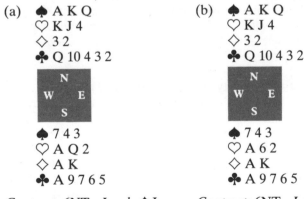

(a) ♠ A K Q
   ♡ K J 4
   ♢ 3 2
   ♣ Q 10 4 3 2

   ♠ 7 4 3
   ♡ A Q 2
   ♢ A K
   ♣ A 9 7 6 5

Contract: 6NT *Lead:* ♠J

(b) ♠ A K Q
   ♡ K J 4
   ♢ 3 2
   ♣ Q 10 4 3 2

   ♠ 7 4 3
   ♡ A 6 2
   ♢ A K
   ♣ A 9 7 6 5

Contract: 6NT *Lead:* ♠J

In (a) 6NT is excellent, so you relax, win the ♠Q and lay down the ♣A. Too late! West discards a diamond and you must give up two tricks to East's remaining ♣ K J.

This play would have been necessary if you had overbid to the poor contract of 7NT, since the ♣K falling singleton is by far your best chance of avoiding a club loser, but cashing the ♣A in 6NT is greedy and careless. Consider the correct thought process.

Question: 'How good is my contract?'
Answer: 'Excellent.'
Question: 'Can anything go wrong?'
Answer: 'Not if clubs break 2–1, but I must give some thought whether it is possible to avoid two club losers if the suit breaks 3–0.'

At this stage you should mentally give each defender in turn ♣ K J 8 and try to work out ways of avoiding a loser. One perfectly good way is to lead a low club from dummy.

If East fails to follow suit you will rise with the ♣A and lead up to dummy's ♣Q.

If East follows with the ♣K or ♣J you can take the ♣A.

If East follows with the ♣8, play the ♣9 from your hand. If West wins this cheaply, the suit must be breaking 2–1, so you have 12 easy tricks.

Can you afford this safety play in hand (b)? That depends on whether you have a heart loser, so it is a good idea to discover this early. Take the ♠A, cash the ♡A and finesse dummy's ♡J.

If the ♡J wins, lead a low club from dummy, intending to insert the ♣9 if East follows with the ♣8.

Alternatively, if the ♡J loses to the ♡Q you now cannot afford to give up a trick in clubs. Your best chance is to cash the ♣A, hoping that one of the defenders holds the ♣K singleton.

Note that a safety play doesn't have to guarantee your contract in order to be worthwhile.

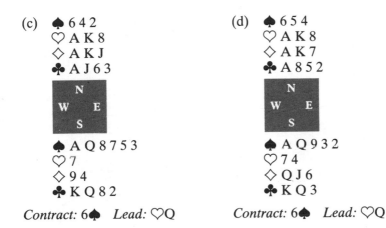

(c) ♠ 6 4 2
     ♡ A K 8
     ♢ A K J
     ♣ A J 6 3

     ♠ A Q 8 7 5 3
     ♡ 7
     ♢ 9 4
     ♣ K Q 8 2

Contract: 6♠ *Lead:* ♡Q

(d) ♠ 6 5 4
     ♡ A K 8
     ♢ A K 7
     ♣ A 8 5 2

     ♠ A Q 9 3 2
     ♡ 7 4
     ♢ Q J 6
     ♣ K Q 3

Contract: 6♠ *Lead:* ♡Q

If you had been in 7♠ with hand (c) you would have had to take the ♡A and finesse the ♠Q, hoping that East has the ♠K doubleton. In the better contract of 6♠ you will succeed comfortably if East has the ♠K singleton, doubleton or tripleton, or if spades break 2–2. Rather than smugly being satisfied you should try to improve on that. Why not cash the ♠A at trick 2? You now succeed also if West started with the ♠K singleton, and you haven't jeopardised your chances if East has the ♠K, because should the ♠A fail to drop the ♠Q you can re-enter dummy and lead up to the ♠Q. You won't succeed if West has ♠ K J x, or spades are 4–0, but there was nothing you could have done about such unfriendly holdings.

With (d) your slam is somewhat less promising. Superficially you can finesse the ♠Q, succeeding if East has ♠ K x or ♠ K x x. However, why not first try a spade from dummy to your ♠9? You can finesse the ♠Q next time so you have lost nothing, and if East was dealt ♠ J 10 x your ♠9 will force out the ♠K. Don't worry about the distributions that give you no chance.

Sometimes a safety play can help you avoid an unwelcome adverse ruff.

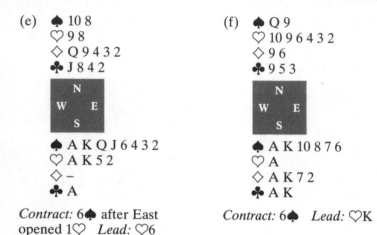

(e) ♠ 10 8
♡ 9 8
◇ Q 9 4 3 2
♣ J 8 4 2

♠ A K Q J 6 4 3 2
♡ A K 5 2
◇ –
♣ A

Contract: 6♠ after East opened 1♡ *Lead:* ♡6

(f) ♠ Q 9
♡ 10 9 6 4 3 2
◇ 9 6
♣ 9 5 3

♠ A K 10 8 7 6
♡ A
◇ A K 7 2
♣ A K

Contract: 6♠ *Lead:* ♡K

In (e) East rises with the ♡10 on West's opening lead, taken by your ♡A. You now have good prospects of making 13 tricks by means of two heart ruffs in dummy, but ask yourself the crucial question: 'What can go wrong?'

Suppose West ruffs your ♡K continuation and switches to a trump. You now have only one trump left in dummy and two losing hearts in your hand. One down! Would it surprise you to be told that your spade slam is laydown? Simply duck a heart at trick 2. The defenders are welcome to switch to a trump, but you can ruff your remaining heart loser in dummy, draw the outstanding trumps and later cash the ♡K.

In (f) the danger of a 4–1 trump break leaving you with a trump loser is far greater than the possibility of the ◇A or ◇K being ruffed, so you can't afford to duck a diamond. But you can do better than ◇ A K, ruffing the ◇2 with the ♠9, allowing East to overruff with the ♠J and return a trump. Instead, cash the ◇ A K, ruff the ◇2 with the ♠Q, re-enter your hand and ruff the last diamond. The defenders can score just one trump trick.

Quiz 10

1) ♠ A Q 7
♡ 6 4
♢ Q J 4
♣ A K 4 3 2

♠ K 8 6
♡ A K 7 5
♢ A K 2
♣ J 10 5

(i) *Contract:* 7NT *Lead:* ♠J
(ii) *Contract:* 6NT *Lead:* ♠J

2) ♠ A 6 3 2
♡ A 9 3
♢ A K 2
♣ A 8 4

♠ J
♡ K Q J 10 7 4
♢ 9 4 3
♣ K Q 6

Contract: 6♡ after West
opened 3♠ *Lead:* ♠K

3) ♠ 9 8 3
♡ A 8 5 2
♢ 9 6 4
♣ 7 4 2

♠ A K Q J 10
♡ –
♢ A K Q 10 2
♣ A K 3

(i) *Contract:* 7♠ *Lead:* ♣Q
(ii) *Contract:* 6♠ *Lead:* ♣Q

4) ♠ –
♡ 6 5 3 2
♢ 4 3
♣ A K Q J 10 6 3

♠ 9 5 4 2
♡ A K Q 4
♢ A 7 2
♣ 5 2

(i) *Contract:* 7♡ *Lead:* ♠A
(ii) *Contract:* 6♡ *Lead:* ♠A

13.   The Safe Hand

(a) ♠ 8 4
     ♡ K 6 2
     ◇ K J 7 4 3
     ♣ A 10 3

(b) ♠ 8 4
     ♡ K 6 2
     ◇ K J 7 4 3
     ♣ A 10 3

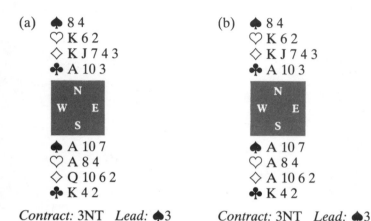

♠ A 10 7
♡ A 8 4
◇ Q 10 6 2
♣ K 4 2

♠ A 10 7
♡ A 8 4
◇ A 10 6 2
♣ K 4 2

Contract: 3NT *Lead:* ♠3   *Contract:* 3NT *Lead:* ♠3

In hand (a) West leads the ♠3 to East's ♠K. Naturally you
withhold your ♠A and East returns the ♠J, West following with
the ♠2 when you again play low. You are forced to take trick 3
with the ♠A, discarding the ♡2 from dummy.

The spades are clearly breaking 5–3, and you have no choice
but to tackle the diamond suit, well aware that you will succeed if
East has the ◇A, but if West has this card he will defeat you with
two more spade tricks.

In (a) there is no point in worrying about the position of the
◇A as you have no way of influencing your fate. Now imagine
you are playing (b), the first three tricks progressing as in (a).
You have a choice of how to play diamonds. All things being
equal the correct way to tackle the diamonds is to play for the
drop, but all things are far from equal!

It isn't only losing the diamond trick that worries you, as 4
diamond tricks will suffice. It is the ability of the defenders to
cash two spade tricks that can sink you. Of course East cannot
cash spade tricks, so that means you don't really mind losing the
lead to East. East is called the *safe hand* and this will affect how

you play the diamonds. The context of the whole hand makes it sensible to cash the $\diamondsuit$A and finesse dummy's $\diamondsuit$J. Even if that loses, you will regain the lead, making nine tricks.

Note that the saying 'Eight ever, nine never' is irrelevant and indeed, dangerous. Ironically, once West is known to have five spades and East only three, it is more likely that East has the $\diamondsuit$Q, but the expert prefers to make a play that seems to disregard the percentages if that safeguards the contract.

Sometimes a hand is 'dangerous' not because it has winners to cash but because it can lead through a vulnerable holding in your hand or in dummy.

(c)   ♠ 7 4
       ♡ A J 5 3
       ◇ A J 3 2
       ♣ 5 4 2

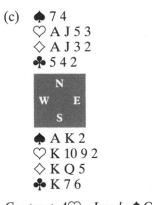

       ♠ A K 2
       ♡ K 10 9 2
       ◇ K Q 5
       ♣ K 7 6

Contract: 4♡ *Lead:* ♠Q

You will make your game irrespective of the position of the ♣A provided East doesn't gain the lead. If East makes a trump trick he can switch to ♣Q from ♣ Q J 8 and the defenders score three club tricks. Therefore, play the ♡2 to dummy's ♡A and lead the ♡J, playing low from your hand unless East covers with the ♡Q. In the fullness of time you will ruff a spade in dummy, discard a club on dummy's fourth diamond and maybe finesse the ♣K for an overtrick.

In the next two hands it seems probable that West has led from
♠ A J 10 x x x x, leaving East with a low doubleton spade. Do you
take trick 1, or allow the ♠J to win?

(d)   ♠ 8
      ♡ A 6 3 2
      ◇ Q J 6 2
      ♣ Q J 10 3

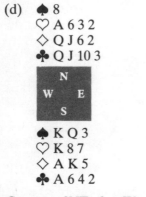

      ♠ K Q 3
      ♡ K 8 7
      ◇ A K 5
      ♣ A 6 4 2

Contract: 3NT after West
opened 3♠ *Lead:* ♠J, East
playing ♠5.

(e)   ♠ 8
      ♡ A 6 3 2
      ◇ Q J 6 2
      ♣ A 6 4 2

      ♠ K Q 3
      ♡ K 8 7
      ◇ A K 5
      ♣ Q J 10 3

Contract: 3NT after West
opened 3♠ *Lead:* ♠J, East
playing ♠5.

The key lies in the club suit. For (d) and (e) you will have to take
a club finesse. If it wins all will be plain sailing, so imagine it loses.

In (d) West will take the trick. You can ensure your contract by
taking the ♠K, entering dummy with the ♡A and running the
♣Q. If West has the ♣K he will be unable to continue spades
without giving you a second stopper in the suit. By winning the
first spade you have made West the safe hand.

In (e) East will take the trick if the club finesse lets you down.
In that case you don't want him to have a spade left to lead
through your ♠ Q x, allowing West to run riot in spades. The
correct play is to duck trick 1. West can persevere with spades,
but he will be unable to regain the lead to cash them as East will
have no spade left if he subsequently takes a trick with the ♣K.

Sometimes there is no immediate 'dangerous' or 'safe' hand, but you need to anticipate an opponent later becoming dangerous. This can effect the timing of your play.

♠ K 6
♡ K 4 3
♢ A Q J 10
♣ 5 4 3 2

♠ A 4
♡ A 5 2
♢ 5 4 3 2
♣ A Q J 10

Contract: 3NT after West opened 3♠   *Lead:* ♠Q

Which minor suit finesse do you take first? Your contract is only in any danger if both minor suit finesses fail.

Suppose you win the ♠A and finesse the ♢Q. It loses to the ♢K and East returns a spade. You now finesse the ♣Q. That loses and West defeats you with a torrent of spades.

What if instead you take the ♠K and finesse the ♣Q? West wins the ♣K, and perseveres with another spade. You finesse the ♢Q unsuccessfully, but East has no spade left to return so your contract is secure.

Quiz 11

1) ♠ 5
  ♡ 7 6 2
  ♢ A Q J 5 4
  ♣ A 7 4 2

```
        N
    W       E
        S
```

  ♠ A K Q 10 6 4 2
  ♡ K 5 3
  ♢ K 7
  ♣ 3

Contract: 4♠ *Lead:* ♣K

2) ♠ 10 9 8
  ♡ 9 4 2
  ♢ A 10 9 3
  ♣ A K 4

```
        N
    W       E
        S
```

  ♠ A Q J
  ♡ A Q 10
  ♢ Q J 4 2
  ♣ 6 5 3

Contract: 3NT *Lead:* ♡5
to East's ♡8

3) ♠ K 9
  ♡ 8 5 2
  ♢ A Q J 10 6 4
  ♣ A 3

```
        N
    W       E
        S
```

  ♠ A 8 5
  ♡ K 6
  ♢ 9 8 5 3
  ♣ K 7 4 2

Contract: 3NT *Lead:* ♠Q

4) ♠ A 10 4 2
  ♡ 7 4
  ♢ A Q 7 2
  ♣ Q J 5

```
        N
    W       E
        S
```

  ♠ K J
  ♡ K Q 6
  ♢ J 10 9 6
  ♣ A K 6 3

Contract: 3NT *Lead:* ♡5
to East's ♡10

14. Trump Management

One of the earliest pieces of advice given to beginners is to 'draw trumps'. A little thought might adjust that advice to 'draw *losing* enemy trumps'.

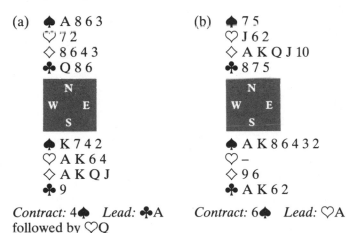

(a) ♠ A 8 6 3
     ♡ 7 2
     ◇ 8 6 4 3
     ♣ Q 8 6

     ♠ K 7 4 2
     ♡ A K 6 4
     ◇ A K Q J
     ♣ 9

Contract: 4♠ *Lead:* ♣A followed by ♡Q

(b) ♠ 7 5
     ♡ J 6 2
     ◇ A K Q J 10
     ♣ 8 7 5

     ♠ A K 8 6 4 3 2
     ♡ –
     ◇ 9 6
     ♣ A K 6 2

Contract: 6♠ *Lead:* ♡A

Playing (a) it would clearly be perverse to cash the ♠ A K and play a third trump if they have broken 3–2 because you want 2 heart ruffs in dummy. However, there is a danger in drawing even two rounds of trumps. Suppose you take the ♡A, cash the ♠ A K (finding trumps 4–1) and ♡K and ruff the ♡4. If East overruffs and cashes his last trump you will be held to 9 tricks. It isn't the overruff that damaged you, but allowing the defenders to cash a master trump, drawing two of yours. To guarantee 10 tricks on a 4–1 break take the ♡A, cash just the ♠A, followed by the ♡K and ruff the ♡4. Your next move will be to return to hand with the ♠K and ruff the fourth heart.

Hand (b) is an exception to the principle of drawing only losing trumps. You ruff the ♡A and cash the ♠ A K, trumps breaking 3–1. You shouldn't turn your attention to diamonds because a defender can choose to ruff at a moment that cuts you off from dummy, leaving you with losing clubs. Having control of all the other suits, you must concede the trump loser immediately, allowing you subsequently to enjoy your diamonds in peace.

With 11 trumps in the combined hands it would seem unlikely that drawing one round can do much harm, but look at (c).

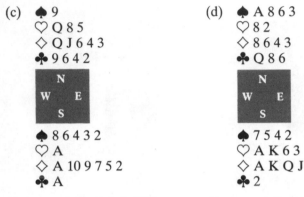

(c) ♠ 9
    ♡ Q 8 5
    ♢ Q J 6 4 3
    ♣ 9 6 4 2

    ♠ 8 6 4 3 2
    ♡ A
    ♢ A 10 9 7 5 2
    ♣ A

Contract: 5♢ Lead: ♣K

(d) ♠ A 8 6 3
    ♡ 8 2
    ♢ 8 6 4 3
    ♣ Q 8 6

    ♠ 7 5 4 2
    ♡ A K 6 3
    ♢ A K Q J
    ♣ 2

Contract: 4♠ Lead: ♡Q

If trumps break 1–1, 12 tricks will present no difficulty, but that doesn't necessarily mean that you are guaranteed 11 if they don't break. If you take the ♣A, cash the ♢A and concede a spade the defender with the ♢K will cash it, leaving you with a second inescapable spade loser if the suit breaks 5–2. Correct play is to duck a spade at trick 2, ruff the club continuation and only then cash the ♢A.

In hand (d) you need a 3–2 trump break to succeed. When you play ♠A followed by another spade the defenders will hold you to 9 tricks by cashing a third round. If you ignore trumps you risk allowing the opponent with the doubleton trump to ruff a winner. To keep tight control you should duck a trump at trick 2. Subsequently you can cash the ♠A, and take two heart ruffs in dummy, using diamonds as entries to your hand.

The 7-card Fit

However desirable it might seem always to play in an 8-card fit, we all sometimes end up playing a suit contract with only 7 trumps. The ability to handle such contracts is the sign of an expert. Perhaps you would rather be in 5♣ with (e) but you must concentrate on fulfilling your heart game.

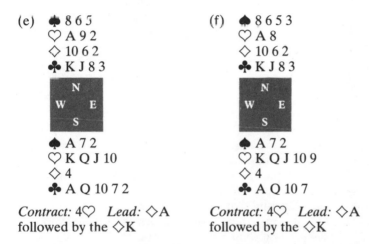

(e) ♠ 8 6 5
    ♡ A 9 2
    ◇ 10 6 2
    ♣ K J 8 3

    ♠ A 7 2
    ♡ K Q J 10
    ◇ 4
    ♣ A Q 10 7 2

Contract: 4♡ *Lead:* ◇A
followed by the ◇K

(f) ♠ 8 6 5 3
    ♡ A 8
    ◇ 10 6 2
    ♣ K J 8 3

    ♠ A 7 2
    ♡ K Q J 10 9
    ◇ 4
    ♣ A Q 10 7

Contract: 4♡ *Lead:* ◇A
followed by the ◇K

The main purpose of a trump suit is to give you *control*, but despite your 10 winners this hand could immediately run out of control if trumps break 4–2. It wouldn't be so bad if you could ruff the ◇K in the hand with 3 trumps, but if you ruff with the 4-card holding your ability to draw the enemy trumps could be fatally damaged. Here the solution is *not* to ruff the second or third tricks, but to discard spades instead. If the defenders persist with a fourth diamond you can ruff it in dummy. You have lost nothing by this manoeuvre, simply exchanging spade losers for diamond losers. Your ten tricks are still available.

It is harder to see it, but the same technique is right for (f). If trumps break 4–2 or 3–3 you will have lost nothing, but if they are 5–1 you will have retained trump control.

(g)   ♠ K 5   (h)   ♠ 7 4
       ♡ 9 6 3 2   ♡ A 8 7 5
       ◇ A 6 3   ◇ J 6 5
       ♣ 9 8 6 5   ♣ A K 3 2

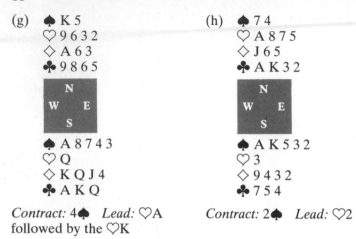

       ♠ A 8 7 4 3   ♠ A K 5 3 2
       ♡ Q   ♡ 3
       ◇ K Q J 4   ◇ 9 4 3 2
       ♣ A K Q   ♣ 7 5 4

Contract: 4♠   *Lead:* ♡A   *Contract:* 2♠   *Lead:* ♡2
followed by the ♡K

In (g) your spade game appears to be an ugly contract, but closer examination shows there is no better resting place available. Provided trumps break 3–3 or 4–2 you should succeed, provided you are not too greedy. You must ruff the ♡K and cash the ♠K and ♣A. This leaves two trumps outstanding. Suppose you try to draw them by playing a third trump. If they are divided you will make 11 tricks, but if they are in the same hand you will be in trouble. The defender will cash them both and settle down to take heart tricks.

This play would have been essential if your contract had been 5♠, but in 4♠ you can afford 2 trump losers, provided you don't lose control. After cashing the ♠K and ♠A take your minor suit winners, allowing the defenders to trump in when it suits them.

Playing (h) you simply appear to be short of tricks. You certainly will be if you try to draw trumps, but you might scramble 8 tricks if you aim to ruff 3 hearts in your hand. Take the ♡A, ruff the ♡5, cash the ♠ A K, enter dummy with the ♣A, ruff the ♡7, cross again with the ♣K and ruff the ♡8. You have taken the first 8 tricks and subsequently the defenders end up trumping each others' winners.

Other Techniques with the Trump Suit

(j) ♠ J 7 5
♡ A 6 4 2
◇ 8 6 4
♣ 10 5 2

(k) ♠ A 8 4 2
♡ A Q 2
◇ A 6 4
♣ K Q J

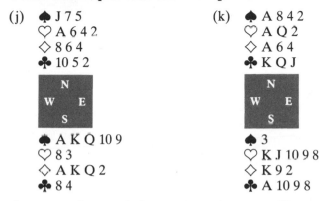

♠ A K Q 10 9
♡ 8 3
◇ A K Q 2
♣ 8 4

♠ 3
♡ K J 10 9 8
◇ K 9 2
♣ A 10 9 8

Contract: 4♠ *Lead:* ♣ A K Q   *Contract:* 7♡ *Lead:* ♠K

Playing (j) it appears that you require diamonds to break 3–3, but if you can envisage the possibility of a diamond ruff in dummy you might improve on that.

Ruff the ♣Q and cash the ♠ A K, noting with pleasure the 3–2 break. Now play the ◇ A K Q. Of course you may suffer a ruff, but in that case you were going to fail anyway as diamonds were not 3–3. If both opponents follow to the third diamond, draw trumps and cash the ◇2. It is possible that the same opponent has 3 trumps and 4 diamonds, in which case he cannot ruff the ◇Q and you will be able to ruff the ◇2 in dummy for your tenth trick.

The same technique might work in (k), but with plenty of entries to dummy a *Dummy Reversal* offers better prospects. The idea is to ruff 3 spades in your hand, using dummy's hearts to draw trumps. Take the ♠A, ruff the ♠2, cash your ♡K, enter dummy with the ♡Q (noting trumps are 3–2), ruff the ♠4, cross again with the ◇A and ruff the ♠8. A club to the ♣J allows you to draw the last outstanding trump with dummy's ♡A and you have 4 more minor suit winners. Note that ruffing 2 spades in your hand achieved nothing, it was ruffing the third spade that gave you the extra trick.

Quiz 12

1) ♠ 9 8
♡ 8 7 3
♢ A 9 6 2
♣ 8 6 3 2

♠ A Q J 10 5
♡ 4 2
♢ K Q J 10
♣ A K

Contract: 4♠ *Lead:* ♡A
followed by ♡K and ♡Q

2) ♠ 9 2
♡ 8 6
♢ 8 4 3
♣ Q J 10 7 3 2

♠ A K Q 8 6
♡ 2
♢ A J 7 6
♣ A K 8

Contract: 4♠ *Lead:* ♡Q
followed by ♡3

3) ♠ K 8 3 2
♡ A 10 7
♢ A 4
♣ K 8 5 2

♠ A J 6 5 4
♡ 6 3
♢ J 7 3 2
♣ A 4

Contract: 4♠ *Lead:* ♣Q

4) ♠ A K Q J
♡ 8 5
♢ A K Q J 10
♣ A 9

♠ 10 3 2
♡ 6 4 3 2
♢ 4 3 2
♣ K 8 2

Contract: 4♠ *Lead:* ♡A

15. Endplays

How many tricks do you expect to make from the layout below?
Spades are trumps and neither opponent has a trump left, but no
high hearts have yet been played.

Consider problem (a), firstly, if South has the lead, and
secondly, if West has the lead.

(a) ♠ J
   ♡ A 10 4

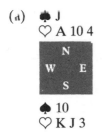

♠ 10
♡ K J 3

If South has the lead South must guess the location of the ♡Q to
make four tricks.

But suppose West is on lead. If West leads a heart South
cannot fail to make three heart tricks. On the other hand, if West
concedes the lead (known as *exiting*) by playing a minor suit,
South can ruff it in hand and discard a heart from dummy, thus
making the two trumps separately. This is called giving declarer a
ruff-and-discard, something defenders avoid if at all possible.

This example seems to go against everything you have hitherto
learned. Up to now you have been presented with the vision of
defenders keen to establish their winners and cash them the
moment you concede the lead. Here we are actually saying that it
is to your advantage if they have the lead, as they are forced to
self-destruct! There are many combinations where, if you can
force your opponents to open up a suit, they will save you a
guess. The trick is to remove all their safe exit cards and then give

them the lead (known as *throwing them in*, or *endplaying* them).

An endplay can be effective in either a suit contract or no-trumps, but it is most common when you have a trump suit because the threat of a ruff-and-discard is lethal. An endplay needs careful preparation.

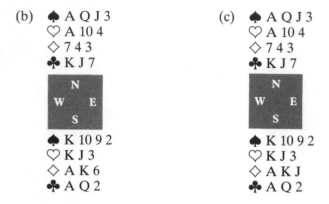

(b)   ♠ A Q J 3
       ♡ A 10 4
       ◇ 7 4 3
       ♣ K J 7

       ♠ K 10 9 2
       ♡ K J 3
       ◇ A K 6
       ♣ A Q 2

(c)   ♠ A Q J 3
       ♡ A 10 4
       ◇ 7 4 3
       ♣ K J 7

       ♠ K 10 9 2
       ♡ K J 3
       ◇ A K J
       ♣ A Q 2

In hand (b) South, in 6♠, takes the ◇Q lead with the ◇A and draws trumps in three rounds. An inexperienced declarer might now try a heart finesse. 50% of the time he will be lucky, and he will never realise that he misplayed the hand. The correct play is to cash the ◇K and ♣ A K Q (otherwise a defender can safely exit with a club). Finally concede the lead with the ◇6. The position is now as in diagram (a) on page 91, ensuring South's success whoever has the ♡Q.

How about (c)? It is exactly the same as (b) except that South has the ◇J rather than the ◇6. Now there is the possibility of making 13 tricks by finding both red suit queens, but if you are in 6♠ that is a snare! If you take a diamond finesse West might win the ◇Q and exit with a diamond, leaving you to guess the position of the ♡Q. It is crucial that if you lose a diamond trick you have no minor suit cards left, forcing the defender to open up the heart suit or concede a ruff-and-discard. You should time the play exactly as in (b), exiting with the ◇J rather than the ◇6. It would be ironic if the extra diamond honour in (c) tempted you to failure.

It helps if you learn to recognise the sort of holdings that are best left for opponents to play.

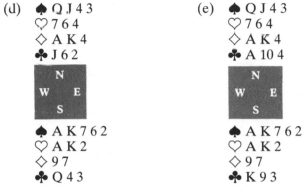

(d) ♠ Q J 4 3
    ♡ 7 6 4
    ♢ A K 4
    ♣ J 6 2

    ♠ A K 7 6 2
    ♡ A K 2
    ♢ 9 7
    ♣ Q 4 3

Contract: 4♠ Lead: ♢Q

(e) ♠ Q J 4 3
    ♡ 7 6 4
    ♢ A K 4
    ♣ A 10 4

    ♠ A K 7 6 2
    ♡ A K 2
    ♢ 9 7
    ♣ K 9 3

Contract: 6♠ Lead: ♢Q

In (d) take the ♢A, draw trumps (say in 3 rounds), eliminate diamonds by cashing the ♢K and ruffing the ♢4, cash the ♡ A K and exit with the ♡2. Suppose West wins and leads a low club. Play low from dummy, and you are guaranteed one trick in the suit.

The endplay on offer in (e) isn't foolproof, but without it your prospects of avoiding a club loser are slim. Draw trumps, eliminate the red suits and endplay the defence with a heart. Your best chance is that the club honours are divided. Suppose West exits with the ♣2. Play the ♣4 from dummy, forcing East to contribute his honour. Capture this with the ♣K and finesse dummy's ♣10.

Note that a clever West with ♣ Q x x might try a deceptive trick by leading the ♣Q, pretending to have ♣ Q J x. The winning play is to take dummy's ♣A and finesse your ♣9, but he had given you a losing option, namely winning with the ♣K and finessing dummy's ♣10. Can you see why you shouldn't be fooled? If West had ♣ Q J x surely the defence would have arranged for East to take the third heart, giving you no chance. Of course it is possible they have made a horrible mess of it, but in general it pays to assume the defenders have performed competently.

So far all the endplays we have seen have been in a side suit, but you can use the 'problem' suit for the endplay.

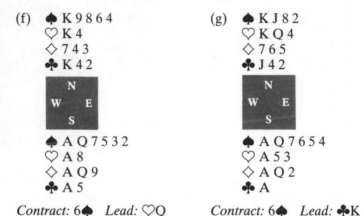

(f)   ♠ K 9 8 6 4   (g)   ♠ K J 8 2
       ♡ K 4   ♡ K Q 4
       ◇ 7 4 3   ◇ 7 6 5
       ♣ K 4 2   ♣ J 4 2

       ♠ A Q 7 5 3 2   ♠ A Q 7 6 5 4
       ♡ A 8   ♡ A 5 3
       ◇ A Q 9   ◇ A Q 2
       ♣ A 5   ♣ A

Contract: 6♠   Lead: ♡Q   *Contract: 6♠   Lead: ♣K*

In (f) win the ♡A, draw trumps, eliminate clubs (ruffing the third round), enter dummy with the ♡K and lead a diamond. If East plays low insert the ◇9. West may win cheaply, but will then be endplayed. It won't help East to jump in with the ◇10 because you will cover it with the ◇Q, again forcing West to lead a diamond or concede a ruff-and-discard.

In (g) the ♣K lead has fatally given away the position of the ♣Q, which you are going to use for an endplay. Take your ♣A, draw trumps ending in dummy, ruff the ♣4, cash the ♡ A K Q and discard the ◇2 on dummy's ♣J.

An endplay doesn't necessarily need the threat of a ruff-and-discard. How do you fancy your prospects of making your heart slam in (h)?

(h) ♠ 8 4
    ♡ K 10 7 5
    ◇ 7 6 4 3
    ♣ K 6 4

    ♠ A K
    ♡ A Q J 8 6 4 3
    ◇ A Q
    ♣ Q 3

(j) ♠ 8 4 3
    ♡ 8 6 4
    ◇ A Q 5 4
    ♣ Q 7 3

    ♠ A 7 6 2
    ♡ A Q
    ◇ K 6 3 2
    ♣ A K 5

Contract: 6♡ after West opened 1♠ *Lead:* ♣Q

Contract: 3NT after West overcalled 1♠ *Lead:* ♠K

There is the ♣A to lose, and the opening bid makes it clear that West has the ◇K, but the contract is still a certainty if you concentrate on what is going on. Take the ♠A, draw trumps and lead the ♣3 from your hand. West cannot take his ♣A without establishing a second club winner for you, so dummy's ♣K wins. Now cash the rest of the trumps and the ♠K, leaving you with 3 cards: the ♣Q and ◇ A Q. What has West retained? Unless he has the ◇K singleton (allowing you to cash the ◇A and ◇Q) he must have the ♣A and ◇ K x. Exit with the ♣Q and West will concede the last two tricks.

Playing (j) you duck the ♠K and take your ♠A when East discards on the spade continuation at trick 2. Next you cash the ◇ A K, but West discards a heart, destroying your hopes of four diamond tricks. The heart finesse doesn't look too promising, so you cash the ♣ A K Q and ◇Q. West follows to the clubs and discards a spade on the ◇Q. You can now ensure your contract by exiting with a spade, forcing West to lead hearts to your advantage.

Quiz 13

1) ♠ 9 3 2
   ♡ A J 6 2
   ◇ K Q 7 5
   ♣ 9 3

```
        N
   W         E
        S
```

   ♠ A K Q
   ♡ 10 5 3
   ◇ A J 10 9 6
   ♣ A 6

Contract: 5◇   *Lead:* ♠J

2) ♠ K Q 6 4
   ♡ K 2
   ◇ A 10 9 8
   ♣ A K J

```
        N
   W         E
        S
```

   ♠ A J 10 8 3
   ♡ A Q
   ◇ K 7 3
   ♣ 8 3 2

Contract: 6♠   *Lead:* ♣10

3) ♠ A 7
   ♡ 9 5 4 3
   ◇ A 8 5 3
   ♣ 7 5 2

```
        N
   W         E
        S
```

   ♠ K 6
   ♡ A J 10 8 7 6 2
   ◇ 4
   ♣ A K J

Contract: 6♡   *Lead:* ♠Q
West has ♡ K Q

4) ♠ 8 6
   ♡ A K 8
   ◇ K 4 3 2
   ♣ Q J 10 5

```
        N
   W         E
        S
```

   ♠ K 7 2
   ♡ 6 3 2
   ◇ A Q 6
   ♣ K 9 7 2

Contract: 3NT after West
opened 1♠   *Lead:* ◇J

16. Counting

Counting Points

If you take time to watch an expect player at the table you will
notice that in those situations which seem to involve a guess he
seems to guess right far more than wrong. He seems quite
prepared to allow his judgement to override such sayings as
'eight ever, nine never', indeed he seems to have an uncanny
knack of finding that vital missing queen. See if you can work out
who has the ◇Q in (a).

(a) ♠ K J 5 3
    ♡ A Q
    ◇ A 10 3 2
    ♣ 9 6 2

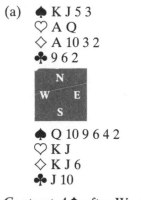

    ♠ Q 10 9 6 4 2
    ♡ K J
    ◇ K J 6
    ♣ J 10

Contract: 4♠ after West
opened 1NT (12–14 HCP)
Lead: ♣ A K Q

(b) ♠ K Q 9 8
    ♡ 10 9 3
    ◇ A 10 9
    ♣ 7 6 2

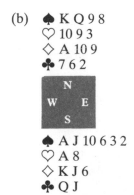

    ♠ A J 10 6 3 2
    ♡ A 8
    ◇ K J 6
    ♣ Q J

Contract: 4♠ after West
opened 1NT (12–14 HCP)
Lead: ♡K

A vague feeling that because West opened he should have the
◇Q isn't good enough. What is required is precise counting of
the enemy points. West has opened a limit bid: 1NT showing
12–14 HCP. He has already shown up with 9, and there are only 6
more missing. West must have the ♠A to make him strong
enough, but that gives him 13 HCP, making it a certainty that
East has the ◇Q.

Of course it is rare for everything to fall into place that easily,
but there is nothing to stop you hunting for information. In (b)
you cannot find out directly who has the ◇Q, but you should be

able to smoke out the heart honours and ♣ A K by playing the other suits. You win the ♡A, draw trumps and exit with a heart. West takes the ♡Q and perseveres with the ♡J, which you ruff. Now exit with the ♣Q. West can do no better than cash the ♣ A K, exiting with the ♣10. He has been seen to hold 13 HCP, so again East has the ◇Q.

You should be particularly alert to counting points if an opponent has made a limit bid during the auction, or has passed and shown up with a significant number of HCP.

Sometimes you are seemingly forced to make a premature guess. In (c) West opened 1♡ and East raised to 3♡, but South ended up in a spade contract. West led the ♡A and East signalled with the ♡Q to show a solid sequence headed by the ♡Q. At trick 2 West continued with the ♡4 to East's ♡10 and East switched to the ♣5. Which club do you play:
(i)   if your contract is 4♠?
(ii)   if your contract is 3♠?

(c)   ♠ 10 9 6 2
        ♡ 9 5
        ◇ A Q 10 8
        ♣ J 8 4

        ♠ A K Q 8 7 5
        ♡ 6 2
        ◇ J 9 4
        ♣ K 10

You would like to know who has the ◇K. If East has it surely West must have the ♣A for his opening bid. On the other hand if West has it then East probably has the ♣A for his 3♡ response. In fact it is up to *you* to decide who has the ◇K, based on the level of your contract.

If you are in 4♠ you have *no chance* unless West has the ◇K, so assume West has it. Therefore East figures to have the ♣A. Rise with your ♣K.

If you are in 3♠ there is *no danger* to your contract unless East has the ◇K, so assume East has it and West has the ♣A. Play the ♣10.

Counting Shape

It almost seems too obvious to be worth saying, but if you can work out how many cards an opponent holds in 3 suits you automatically know his length in the fourth suit. Opportunities to count shape are by no means uncommon.

(d)   ♠ 10
      ♡ 5 2
      ◇ A Q J 9
      ♣ A 8 7 6 4 3

(e)   ♠ A 4
      ♡ 8 4 3 2
      ◇ 8 5 4 3
      ♣ K J 10

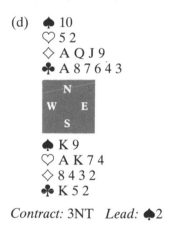

(d)
    ♠ K 9
    ♡ A K 7 4
    ◇ 8 4 3 2
    ♣ K 5 2

(e)
    ♠ K Q 10 9 5
    ♡ J 6
    ◇ J 9 6 2
    ♣ A Q

Contract: 3NT   *Lead:* ♠2

Contract: 2♠   *Lead:* ◇10
after East opened 1NT and
West signed off in 2♡.

In (d) you open 1NT, speculatively raised to 3NT by North. West leads the ♠2 (fourth highest), your ♠K taking the trick. You try the ♣A and ♣K, West showing out.

What is going on? West has led from a 4-card spade suit and has a singleton club. Since he would surely have preferred to lead a 5-card suit his shape appears to be 4–4–4–1. You need 4 diamond tricks, so start by finessing the ◇J, then return to your hand with the ♡A for a finesse of the ◇9. East discards a spade, allowing you to use the ♡K as an entry for a final, marked diamond finesse.

In (e) West leads from the doubleton ♢10, East taking the first 3 tricks with the ♢ Q A K. East then cashes the ♡K and continues with a heart to West's ♡Q. You ruff West's ♡A at trick 6, East discarding a club. East started with just 5 red cards, so remembering his 1NT opening bid he is likely to be 4–4 in the black suits. You cannot work out for sure who has the ♠J, but best play is to assume that East has ♠ J x x x. Enter dummy with the ♠A and finesse your ♠10.

Finally we show an excellent example of a declarer who initially needed to find the ♣Q for his no-trump grand slam, but turned it into a certainty.

(f)

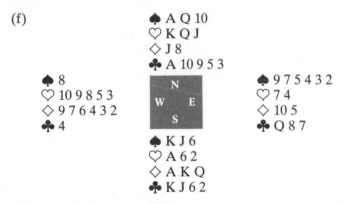

```
                    ♠ A Q 10
                    ♡ K Q J
                    ♢ J 8
                    ♣ A 10 9 5 3
  ♠ 8                              ♠ 9 7 5 4 3 2
  ♡ 10 9 8 5 3          N          ♡ 7 4
  ♢ 9 7 6 4 3 2     W       E      ♢ 10 5
  ♣ 4                   S          ♣ Q 8 7
                    ♠ K J 6
                    ♡ A 6 2
                    ♢ A K Q
                    ♣ K J 6 2
```

Contract: 7NT   *Lead:* ♡10

Declarer took the ♡10 lead in dummy with the ♡K and decided to put off the fateful club guess for as long as possible. He cashed 3 spades, 2 more hearts and 3 diamonds, carefully watching the defenders' cards. By trick 10 he knew everything. West had started with 6 diamonds, 5 hearts and a singleton spade. Therefore he held precisely one club. South could confidently enter dummy with the ♣A, in case West's singleton club was the ♣Q, and finesse the ♣J.

Quiz 14

1) ♠ 8 6 3
♡ 9 5 4
◇ A K 4
♣ K Q 7 3

♠ K Q 9 4 2
♡ J 10
◇ Q J 7
♣ A J 4

Contract: 4♠ West
opened 1♡
Lead: ♡ A K Q

2) ♠ 6 4 3 2
♡ 9 6 3
◇ 7 6 3 2
♣ A 7

♠ A K Q J 9 8
♡ A
◇ A K Q 10
♣ 9 6

Contract: 6♠ West opened 5♣
Lead: ♣K. You play dummy's
♣A and East discards the ♡K.

3) ♠ Q 9 6 2
♡ 10 7 3
◇ 8 7 2
♣ A Q J

♠ A K 10 8 7 5
♡ K J
◇ 9 4 3
♣ 10 4

(i) *Contract:* 2♠   (ii) *Contract:* 3♠
For (i) and (ii): West opened 1NT *(12–14 HCP)*.
Lead: ◇ A K J overtaken by East's ◇Q. East returns the ♡4.

17. Loser-on-loser Play

Most players never give much thought to the role of losers. They are undesirables, to be ruffed or discarded if at all possible. However there are a whole series of plays based on the idea of using your loser for its natural purpose, to lose a trick. The idea is that you exchange one losing card for another, with the hope that this will benefit you in some other way. You have seen in chapter 13 how declarer can protect a fragile trump holding by discarding losers rather than ruffing. Many endplays are also executed by playing a loser in one suit and discarding a loser in another suit (see hand (g) on page 94). Consider (a).

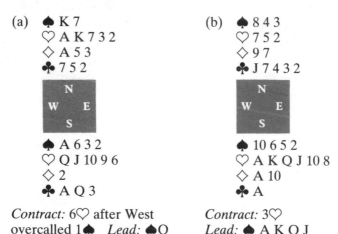

(a)   ♠ K 7
     ♡ A K 7 3 2
     ◇ A 5 3
     ♣ 7 5 2

     ♠ A 6 3 2
     ♡ Q J 10 9 6
     ◇ 2
     ♣ A Q 3

Contract: 6♡ after West
overcalled 1♠   *Lead:* ♠Q

(b)   ♠ 8 4 3
     ♡ 7 5 2
     ◇ 9 7
     ♣ J 7 4 3 2

     ♠ 10 6 5 2
     ♡ A K Q J 10 8
     ◇ A 10
     ♣ A

Contract: 3♡
Lead: ♠ A K Q J

If trumps break 2–1 you can avoid taking the club finesse by taking the ♠K, drawing trumps, and starting a cross-ruff: ◇A, diamond ruff, ♠A, spade ruff, diamond ruff. Now lead your last spade and throw a club, endplaying West.

In (b) it is easy to see that if you ruff the fourth spade in dummy East might overruff, leaving you with a diamond loser. Ruffing with the ♡7 will be successful if West has the ♡9, but there is no reason for you to take this gamble. Allow West to make his ♠J, discarding dummy's ◇7. Later you can ruff a diamond in dummy without fear of being overruffed. You have exchanged a diamond loser for a spade loser, to safeguard your ruff.

In our next two examples the idea is to build winners out of cards that initially might seem like losers.

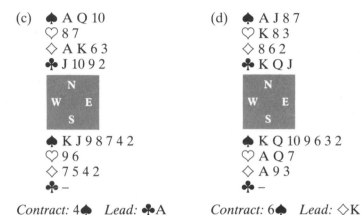

(c)
♠ A Q 10
♡ 8 7
◇ A K 6 3
♣ J 10 9 2

♠ K J 9 8 7 4 2
♡ 9 6
◇ 7 5 4 2
♣ –

Contract: 4♠ Lead: ♣A

(d)
♠ A J 8 7
♡ K 8 3
◇ 8 6 2
♣ K Q J

♠ K Q 10 9 6 3 2
♡ A Q 7
◇ A 9 3
♣ –

Contract: 6♠ Lead: ◇K

Most players would find it hard to conceive of a useful purpose for dummy's rather mediocre clubs, but the club intermediates mean you can guarantee your contract without worrying about the diamond break. Trump the ♣A, draw trumps ending in dummy and discard the ♡6 on the ♣J. West wins the trick with the ♣Q and tries to cash hearts but you can ruff the second heart. Next cross to dummy with the ◇A and discard a diamond on the ♣10. Later dummy's ♣9 provides a parking place for your other losing diamond. You have lost just 2 clubs and a heart.

In (d) without the diamond lead you could have thrown diamonds leisurely on clubs without worrying about who has the ♣A. Unfortunately the ◇K lead has exposed your weakness, so your contract is far from secure. You should draw trumps ending in dummy and call for the ♣K. You intend to take a *ruffing finesse*. Like any other finesse, you require one particular opponent to have a vital missing card. If East has the ♣A he is helpless. Covering the ♣K with the ♣A allows you to ruff, re-enter dummy and discard diamond losers on the ♣ Q J. If he declines to cover you intend to throw losing diamonds from your hand anyway.

In the final example we show all four hands. Superficially declarer has 10 tricks: 5 spades (with the suit breaking 3–2), 4 clubs and the ♡A. However, West starts with the ◇ A K and continues with the ◇8, ruffed by East with the ♠10. How should declarer react to this?

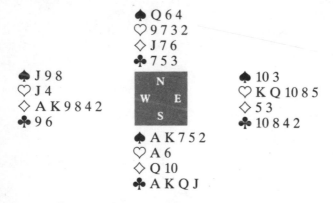

```
              ♠ Q 6 4
              ♡ 9 7 3 2
              ◇ J 7 6
              ♣ 7 5 3
♠ J 9 8                        ♠ 10 3
♡ J 4         N                ♡ K Q 10 8 5
◇ A K 9 8 4 2  W   E           ◇ 5 3
♣ 9 6             S            ♣ 10 8 4 2
              ♠ A K 7 5 2
              ♡ A 6
              ◇ Q 10
              ♣ A K Q J
```

If South overruffs he is doomed to lose a trump trick and a heart. East's clever ruff with his high trump is called an *Uppercut*, an attempt to promote trump winners for partner. Fortunately declarer has an equally subtle counter. Instead of making the reflex overruff, he discards a losing heart. Now his remaining trumps are adequate to draw West's spades without further mishap.

If you are threatened with an uppercut, consider whether a loser-on-loser play might serve you better than overruffing.

Quiz 15

1) ♠ 7 6 5
   ♡ K 4 3
   ◇ 8 3
   ♣ K 6 4 3 2

   ♠ A 8 2
   ♡ A Q J 10 2
   ◇ A
   ♣ A Q 10 9

Contract: 6♡   Lead: ◇J

2) ♠ J 10 9
   ♡ A Q 8
   ◇ A J 10 9
   ♣ A K 6

   ♠ A K Q 8 7 4 3
   ♡ 6 2
   ◇ 8
   ♣ 9 7 4

Contract: 6♠   Lead: ♡7

3) ♠ Q 10 8 7 4 2
   ♡ A K 8 4
   ◇ 7 6 2
   ♣ –

   ♠ A K J 6 3
   ♡ –
   ◇ A J 9 5 3
   ♣ K 8 2

Contract: 6♠   Lead: ♣Q

4) ♠ K Q 9 7
   ♡ A Q J
   ◇ A Q J
   ♣ 9 5 4

   ♠ A J 8 6 4 3 2
   ♡ 7
   ◇ 9 7
   ♣ K 3 2

Contract: 4♠   Lead: ◇6

18. The Opening Lead

For beginners, defence is usually considered to be the hardest skill in which to attain adequacy. Since you can't see your partner's hand it is very difficult to co-ordinate the combined campaign. It is not surprising that beginners' books feel it is necessary to quote 'guidelines'. The trouble is that frequently these guidelines contradict each other. It is not too helpful to be told that you should 'lead your longest suit against no-trumps', but 'never lead a suit bid by declarer' if your only long suit has been bid by declarer. Much of the time you don't have a convenient lead. What would you lead with the West hand below after the auction shown?

	SOUTH	NORTH
♠ Q 10 8 3 2		
♡ 4	1♠	2♣
◇ A J 2	2♡	3♡
♣ J 7 6 4	4♡	

If you sit around looking for a 'textbook' lead you will be disappointed. Therefore you should work from the opposite standpoint. Which leads can you rule out?

A spade from ♠ Q 10 8 3 2, declarer's first suit, is very likely to waste a trick and help declarer establish spades.

Leading from your miserable club holding is pointless. Declarer has at most 4 minor suit cards in his hand. Don't let him discard losing diamonds on dummy's club winners.

A trump lead has a lot to recommend it when the opposition are likely to be in a 4–4 fit with cross-ruffing potential, but there are two reasons to avoid a heart lead. Firstly, a singleton trump means that partner is quite likely to have a holding like ♡ Q x x x, or ♡ J x x x, and your lead is likely to expose the layout. Secondly, your spade length means that if declarer tries to ruff spades in dummy your partner may be able to overruff.

That leaves a diamond. Yes, you have been advised not to cash unsupported aces, but it is the only unbid suit and there is a very real danger that any diamond winners may disappear unless you take them soon. The main point is that having ruled out everything else you are left with a diamond as the least of evils.

Of course leading the $\diamond$A might be wrong. The important thing is that you tackle difficult decisions such as this logically. Nobody gets every opening lead right. The clear thinker gets more right than wrong, and if he does get it wrong he doesn't panic. Frequently the sight of dummy and the cards played to trick 1 make you wish you could start all over again, but you must keep a clear head and plan again from where you are. What you must avoid at all costs is the habit of so many defenders of switching wildly from one suit to another under the misapprehension that they must *do something* to redeem the lead and defeat the contract. We cannot say that *you* tend to try to do too much to defeat contracts, but that is true of most defenders. Perhaps it is based on a misguided work ethic, that somehow you are being lazy if you just sit back and do nothing. Experience suggests that far more contracts can be defeated by passive defence than is generally realised. This is particularly true when defending against part-scores. If your opening lead or switch concedes a vital trick there is no way of recovering it. On the other hand, if you fail to find a successful attacking lead you often regain the lead frequently enough to recover.

Listening to the Bidding

You may have noticed that in the above example, the bidding and the state of your hand played a major part in your decision. The likelihood of partner having four trumps and being able to overruff dummy, declarer's minor suit shortage, and the fear that your unhelpful club holding may mean dummy's suit is strong contributed to the decision to lead the $\diamond$A. You should also be aware that the major suits seem to be breaking badly for declarer, and he may have some nasty shocks in store. If he has bid to game with minimum values he may well struggle, suggesting that you should try to avoid giving him cheap tricks.

You can frequently form an educated view from the bidding as to whether declarer is likely to find his contract easy or difficult. Consider the West hand shown below after auctions (i) and (ii).

♠ 4	(i)	SOUTH	NORTH	(ii)	SOUTH	NORTH
♡ K J 9 6 2		1♡	1♠		1♠	3♡
◇ A J 7 2		1NT	2NT		3NT	
♣ 8 6 4		3NT				

In (i) declarer has just about staggered into game. 1NT showed 15–16 points, yet even with this precise information North could only invite game. It sounds as though South has 16 points and North 9. Moreover, everything is lying badly for declarer. Both majors are splitting horribly, your hearts are placed after declarer's heart suit, and partner may well have spades hovering over dummy's spades. Declarer's finesses won't work and he is surely booked for defeat, provided you don't hand it to him on a plate. We recommend a passive club lead, having doubled first!

Auction (ii) is totally different. Firstly, the bidding suggests North/South have plenty to spare for their game. Secondly, if South takes spade finesses through your partner, or heart finesses through you, they will work. You are unlikely to beat this contract whatever you do, but you may have some chance if partner has ◇ K x x x x, declarer holds ◇ Q 10 9 and dummy has a singleton diamond. Now an attacking lead is essential, and once you decide that, it pays to lead the suit that requires least help from partner (or the suit in which you can contribute most). Try the ◇2.

What do you lead with this West hand after the auction below?

♠ 8 6 4	SOUTH	NORTH
♡ J 6 3	1◇	1♡
◇ 6 5 3 2	1NT	3NT
♣ K 7 4		

North may or may not have values to spare, but your red suit holdings suggest that you are unlikely to have any unpleasant shocks for declarer. Your best chance must be to find partner's long suit. Once you have decided on an attacking lead, a club is clear-cut. If partner has long clubs your ♣K may provide vital assistance. In spades you can offer no help. Look at it another way. Suppose you find partner with Q J 5 3 2 of the suit you lead and an ace. In clubs that will defeat the contract. In spades. it won't.

There is, of course, one more clue guiding you away from a spade lead. Partner failed to overcall 1♡ with 1♠. It would have been safer for him to bid spades at the one level than clubs at the two level, so his spades are unlikely to be good enough.

Entries

On lead against 3NT with hand (a) below, you should have great reservations about a spade lead. The lack of entries to your hand suggests that even if you do find partner with strong enough spades to establish spade length winners, you are unlikely to gain the lead to cash your spades. It is better to aim for partner's suit, and since you can offer most help in clubs you should lead the ♣2.

Of course (b) is different. With so many outside entries you can lead the ♠3, plugging away at spades whenever you regain the lead, and hopefully score length tricks.

(a)	♠ J 9 6 3 2	(b)	♠ J 9 6 3 2	SOUTH	NORTH
	♡ 9 5		♡ A 5	1NT	3NT
	◇ 8 6 3		◇ A Q 3		
	♣ J 6 2		♣ 10 6 3		

It is worth commenting that when aiming for a ruff against a suit contract exactly the opposite logic applies.

(c)	♠ 10 6 3	(d)	♠ A 6 3	SOUTH	NORTH
	♡ 2		♡ 2	1♠	3♠
	◇ J 9 6 3		◇ K 9 6 3	4♠	
	♣ 10 8 5 4 2		♣ A Q 9 5 2		

A heart lead is excellent with (c). Hopefully partner has entries, and as you have the excellent holding of 3 tiny trumps it is not impossible that you might take the first 4 tricks, including 2 heart ruffs.

How about (d)? The prospect of partner having an entry is negligible. The most likely outcome of a heart lead is to help declarer find partner's ♡Q. Lead a trump, the ♠3.

The worse your hand, the more suitable it is for seeking a ruff.

Which Card to Lead

In making an opening lead you should clearly address the question of what you are trying to achieve. Sometimes clear thinking will suggest an unexpected choice of card in the suit.

What do you lead with the West hand below after each of the auctions shown?

♠ A K 6 3 2	(i)	SOUTH	NORTH	(ii)	SOUTH	NORTH
♡ 9 6		1NT	3NT		1♡	3♡
◇ 9 6 2					4♡	
♣ 10 6 4						

In (i) you want to concede any spade loser early, hope partner has an entry and subsequently make spade length tricks. If partner has a holding like ♠ Q x you don't want to block the suit. Lead the ♠3.

In (ii) you want to take two quick spades and perhaps give partner a ruff. Lead the ♠A.

What is your choice of lead from these hands after the auction shown?

(e)	♠ A K 10 9 2	(f)	♠ A K 10 9 2	SOUTH	NORTH
	♡ 8 4		♡ 8 4	1NT	3NT
	◇ 9 8 3		◇ A 8 3		
	♣ 9 4 2		♣ 9 4 2		

From (e) lead the ♠10 in order to retain communication with partner. The spades are identical in (f), but you possess the ♢A. Partner is less likely to have an entry, and you are in a position to bring in spades for just one loser if one defender has ♠ Q x and the other ♠ J x x x, provided you start with the ♠A.

How about this hand?

	SOUTH	NORTH
♠ J 7 2		
♡ 6 3		1♡
♢ K Q J 4 2	3♣	3♢
♣ A 4 3	3NT	

Declarer clearly has points to spare, and your club holding holds no terrors for him. Your only chance seems to be in the diamond suit, but with dummy announcing a 4-card diamond suit your ♢4 won't win the fourth round of the suit. You require partner to hold something like ♢ 10 x, so lead a low diamond to avoid blocking the suit.

Attacking Leads

Some auctions simply cry out for an attacking lead.

(i)	SOUTH	NORTH	(ii)	SOUTH	NORTH	(iii)	SOUTH	NORTH
		3♣		3NT (1)	No		1♠	3♣
	3NT	No					3♠	4♠
							6♠	No

(1) Solid 7-card minor with no other A or K.

In (i) North has long clubs, and South probably intends to use them. Set up your own winners with an attacking lead.

In (ii) South has 7 tricks, so you must hope he has a weakness you can exploit. Lead an ace if you have one, allowing you to inspect dummy, while retaining the lead.

(iii) is a typical suit slam auction. With long black suits declarer should have ample tricks, unless you can build two first. Leading from a side suit such as K x x x, hoping partner has the queen or ace, is reasonable.

Quiz 16

In each of the example below you are given a hand and two auctions at *love all*. What do you lead?

1) ♠ K Q 8 5 2
   ♡ A 7
   ◇ J 5 3
   ♣ J 9 4

(i)	SOUTH	NORTH	(ii)	SOUTH	NORTH
	1NT	3NT		1♡	2♡
				2NT	4♡

2) ♠ K J 6 3 2
   ♡ 5
   ◇ K J 6 3
   ♣ 9 8 7

(i)	SOUTH	NORTH	(ii)	SOUTH	NORTH
	1NT	2♣		1NT	2♣
	2♠	2NT		2♡	3NT
	3NT				

3) ♠ A Q J 6 2
   ♡ J 10 9
   ◇ A J 6 4
   ♣ 5

(i)	SOUTH	NORTH	(ii)	SOUTH	NORTH
	1♠	2♣		1♣	1◇
	2NT	3NT		2NT	3NT

4) ♠ K 10 6 2
   ♡ 9 8 6
   ◇ 9 4
   ♣ J 8 5 2

(i)	SOUTH	NORTH	(ii)	SOUTH	NORTH
	1♣	1♠		1◇	1♡
	2NT	3NT		2NT	3NT

5) ♠ A 8 2
   ♡ 3
   ◇ J 8 3 2
   ♣ J 10 9 6 3

(i)	SOUTH	NORTH	(ii)	SOUTH	NORTH
	1♠	3♠		1♠	3♠
	4♠			6♠	

6) ♠ A 9 8
   ♡ K 8 4 3
   ◇ 7 6 5 3
   ♣ 6 2

(i)	SOUTH	NORTH	(ii)	SOUTH	NORTH
	1♠	2◇		3NT (1)	No
	2♠	3♣			
	3♠	5♠			
	6♠				

(1) Solid minor. No other A or K.

7) ♠ 9 8
   ♡ 8 7 5 4 3
   ◇ A 5 4
   ♣ J 8 4

(i)	SOUTH	NORTH	(ii)	SOUTH	NORTH
	1♠	2♡		1♣	1♡
	3♡	4♣		1♠	3♣
				5♣	

19. Manipulating the Trump Suit

Leading a Trump

There is a saying in bridge: 'When in doubt, lead a trump'. Like most sayings it is all too frequently used as an excuse for mental torpor.

Firstly, there are a number of trump holdings that make very unsuitable leads. If you have Q x x or J x x x clearly leading the suit is likely to result in your never making a trick with your honour. Secondly, it is true that a trump lead from you is likely to squander a trick if your partner has one of these holdings. If you have a singleton trump it is highly probable that partner has such a holding, hence the statement in chapter 18 that a singleton trump generally doesn't make a good lead.

A trump lead from a low doubleton or tripleton is usually harmless (though hard luck if you trap partner's queen). From A x x lead the lowest. Firstly, this avoids crashing partner's singleton honour. Secondly, if partner has a low doubleton and regains the lead he can return his last trump, enabling you to draw two more rounds. A trump lead from K x x tends to be safe because if the king is placed after the ace it will still make a trick.

There are certain types of auction which should make you strongly consider a trump lead.

(i) SOUTH	NORTH	(ii) SOUTH	NORTH	(iii) SOUTH	NORTH
1♡	1NT	1♡	1♠	1♣	1♢
2♢		2♢	2♡	1♠	2♠
		3♢	5♢	4♠	

(iv) SOUTH	WEST	NORTH	EAST
			1♡
1♠	2♡	2♠	3♢
No	4♡	4♠	Dbl
No	No	No	

Auctions (i) and (ii) suggest declarer might make tricks by ruffing hearts in dummy.

In (i) South has shown at least 5 hearts and 4 diamonds. North's failure to give preference to 2♡ suggests he might have 3 diamonds and a singleton heart.

In (ii) North initially gave preference to 2♡, but subsequently preferred diamonds when South showed 5–5 shape. He almost certainly has a poor doubleton heart and 3 diamonds. Be especially inclined to lead a trump if you have a strong heart holding positioned after declarer.

In auction (iii) you might fancy a lead in hearts, the unbid suit, but the auction suggests a cross-ruff might be successful for declarer. There is a case for a trump lead if you have a suitable holding.

In auction (iv) East/West clearly expected to make 4♡ and North/South are sacrificing in 4♠ doubled. It sounds as though the defenders have most of the high cards, so declarer's only conceivable salvation will come in a cross-ruff. It often pays to lead a trump against an enemy sacrifice contract.

Playing a Forcing Defence

Try to work out how the defenders can beat 4♡ in this hand.

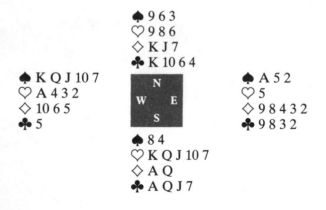

```
                    ♠ 9 6 3
                    ♡ 9 8 6
                    ♢ K J 7
                    ♣ K 10 6 4
♠ K Q J 10 7                              ♠ A 5 2
♡ A 4 3 2          N                      ♡ 5
♢ 10 6 5        W     E                   ♢ 9 8 4 3 2
♣ 5                S                      ♣ 9 8 3 2
                    ♠ 8 4
                    ♡ K Q J 10 7
                    ♢ A Q
                    ♣ A Q J 7
```

Suppose West leads his singleton club. Declarer takes the ♣A, plays 3 rounds of diamonds discarding the ♠4 and attacks trumps. The ♠A will provide an entry for a club ruff, but the defenders will make no further trick.

Now see what happens if the defence starts off with 3 rounds of spades. South ruffs and turns his attention to trumps, but West withholds his ♡A on the first and second round. What can South do now? If he perseveres with a third round of trumps West swoops in with the ♡A and plays a spade, forcing South to ruff with his last trump. South has now lost trump control. Alternatively South may abandon trumps, but West can then ruff a club.

When you have 4 or more trumps it often pays to lead your longest side-suit. You are effectively hoping the bad trump break will prevent declarer drawing trumps while retaining control, thus reducing the hand to no-trump status, and the logic of leading your longest suit is exactly the same as against a no-trump contract.

Special Signals

In the next hand West leads the ◇4 to dummy's ◇2 and your ◇A. How are you going to defeat this contract?

♠ A 9 7 3
♡ K Q
◇ K Q 9 7 2
♣ K Q

North South Game
Dealer: North

SOUTH	WEST	NORTH	EAST
		1◇	No
1♠	No	4♠	No
No	No		

♠ 8 6
♡ A 7 4 2
◇ A 8 5 3
♣ 9 6 2

The ◇4 is clearly a singleton, so hopefully you should take the first 4 tricks: the ◇A, a diamond ruff, the ♡A and another diamond ruff. There is only one snag in this. After giving West his ruff how can you persuade him to switch to a heart rather than to a club?

You can use the size of the diamond you return to indicate *suit preference*. Normally a high card shows interest in a suit, while a low card discourages, but it is obvious here that such signalling is redundant. In that case *suit preference* signals (called McKenney) apply. West could not seriously imagine that a trump switch was sensible, so that leaves a choice between hearts and clubs. A high diamond return (the ◇8) would ask for a switch to the higher ranking suit (hearts) while a low diamond (the ◇3) would request a club.

The ◇8 leads to a ruff, a heart back and a second diamond ruff as declarer has:

♠ K Q 10 5 2   ♡ J 6 3   ◇ J 10 6   ♣ A 5

In the next example West leads the ♠K, and naturally enough East discourages with the ♠2. However, the ♠K holds the trick and West then continues with the ♠A. The ♠A is the natural card to lead from ♠ A K. What do you make of that?

♠ 9 7 3
♡ A Q 3
◇ K J 2
♣ K Q 4 2

Love all
Dealer: North

SOUTH	WEST	NORTH	EAST
		1♣	No

♠ 8 6 4 2
♡ 8 5
◇ A 7 4 3
♣ 9 5 3

SOUTH	WEST	NORTH	EAST
1♡	No	1NT	No
4♡	No	No	No

Partner has played the spades out of order in order to show you he has a doubleton, a conventional signal which is used infrequently but which is very descriptive when it does occur.

You can see the way to defeat this contract by means of the ◇A and a spade ruff, but you must persuade West to switch to a diamond rather than a club. West will be looking for a suit preference signal (it would clearly be pointless for you to encourage a spade continuation when you know he hasn't got any), so play the ♠8. Declarer has:

♠ Q J 10 5   ♡ K J 10 4 3 2   ◇ Q   ♣ A 7

In the next example partner again leads a singleton, the ♣4, but sadly you can't give him an immediate ruff.

♠ Q 10 6 4
♡ Q
♢ 8 4 2
♣ A K Q J 2

♠ K J
♡ A J 7 3
♢ J 10 7
♣ 10 9 7 3

	Game all		
Dealer: North			
SOUTH	WEST	NORTH	EAST
		1♣	No
1♠	No	3♠	No
4♠	No	No	No

Dummy's ♣A wins trick 1, the ♠4 is led to South's ♠A and a second spade to your ♠K. You would be wise to cash the ♡A, but do you aim for a club ruff or switch to a diamond? The question really is: 'Has West got another trump?' You need to have watched the trumps he played. A 'high-low' order is called a *Trump Peter*, and shows exactly 3 trumps and a desire to ruff something. In this case he followed in the order ♠3, ♠7, showing a doubleton. You must switch to the ♢J as South has:

♠ A 9 8 5 2   ♡ K 10 2   ♢ K 6   ♣ 8 6 5

Trump Promotions

In the hand below West cashes the ♢ A K, South following suit with the ♢5 and ♢Q. West then perseveres with the ♢2. How should East defend?

♠ 8 7 5 4
♡ A K Q 4
♢ J 7 3
♣ A K

♠ J 2
♡ J 7 3
♢ 9 6
♣ 10 8 6 5 3 2

	North South Game		
Dealer: North			
SOUTH	WEST	NORTH	EAST
		1♡	No
1♠	2♢	3♠	No
4♠	No	No	No

It is obviously right to ruff out the $\diamond$J, but did it occur to you to ruff with the $\spadesuit$J? West has the $\spadesuit$ K Q doubleton, so if declarer is forced to waste his $\spadesuit$A on overruffing the $\spadesuit$J West makes two trump tricks. Declarer has:

$\spadesuit$ A 10 9 6 3 $\heartsuit$ 10 6 2 $\diamond$ Q 5 $\clubsuit$ Q J 4

It is usually right for a defender to ruff with a trump honour that cannot conceivably be put to any other use, called an *Uppercut*, in the hope that declarer's overruff promotes trump tricks for partner. You may remember from page 104 that declarer sometimes has the counter of discarding a loser rather than overruffing, so the defenders should try to cash their side-suit winners first.

The next example shows it tends to be wrong for a defender to overruff with a certain trump trick. West leads the $\clubsuit$9, allowing East to start the defence with the $\clubsuit$Q and $\clubsuit$A. East persists with the $\clubsuit$K, ruffed by South with the $\spadesuit$J.

	$\spadesuit$ 8 6 3	*Love all*			
	$\heartsuit$ A Q	*Dealer:* North			
	$\diamond$ A Q J 5 2	SOUTH	WEST	NORTH	EAST
	$\clubsuit$ 10 4 3			1$\diamond$	2$\clubsuit$
$\spadesuit$ A 9 5		2$\spadesuit$	No	3$\spadesuit$	No
$\heartsuit$ 10 7 6 5 2	N W E S	4$\spadesuit$	No	No	No
$\diamond$ 10 4 3					
$\clubsuit$ 9 2					

If West overruffs the $\spadesuit$J with the $\spadesuit$A declarer's remaining $\spadesuit$ K Q will enable him to draw trumps without further loss, fulfilling his game contract as he has:

$\spadesuit$ K Q J 7 4 $\heartsuit$ K 8 3 $\diamond$ K 7 6 $\clubsuit$ J 6

If instead West discards a loser, he will come to two trump tricks if East has any spade honour. West didn't know East had the $\spadesuit$10, but he had no obvious reason for overruffing, and he should discard a loser without too much agonising.

Quiz 17

1)

	♠ 8 6 3	*North South Game*			
	♡ K Q J 10	*Dealer:* North			
	♢ Q J 7	SOUTH	WEST	NORTH	EAST
	♣ A K 2			1♡	No
♠ J 5 2	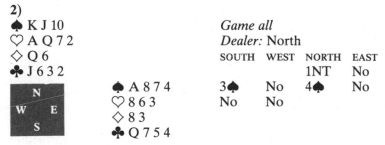	1♠	2♢	No	No
♡ A 9		3♣	No	4♠	No
♢ A K 8 6 3 2		No	No		
♣ 7 5					

West starts the defence with ♢ A K, East following suit with the ♢9 and ♢4. How should West continue?

2)

♠ K J 10		*Game all*			
♡ A Q 7 2		*Dealer:* North			
♢ Q 6		SOUTH	WEST	NORTH	EAST
♣ J 6 3 2				1NT	No
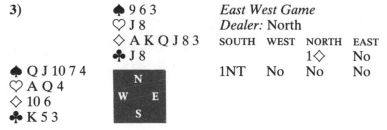	♠ A 8 7 4	3♠	No	4♠	No
	♡ 8 6 3	No	No		
	♢ 8 3				
	♣ Q 7 5 4				

West starts with the ♢ A K, followed by the ♢7 ruffed in dummy. How should East defend?

3)

	♠ 9 6 3	*East West Game*			
	♡ J 8	*Dealer:* North			
	♢ A K Q J 8 3	SOUTH	WEST	NORTH	EAST
	♣ J 8			1♢	No
♠ Q J 10 7 4		1NT	No	No	No
♡ A Q 4					
♢ 10 6					
♣ K 5 3					

West leads the ♠Q, overtaken by East's ♠K. East returns the ♠A at trick 2. Which card should West play?

20. Defensive Counting

Chapter 16 showed you how declarer can use clues available from the defenders' bidding and cards played to help him peep into their hands. Of course the defenders can use the same ideas, and since the declaring side has usually done more bidding there are frequently more clues available. When you are declarer there are many different techniques available, but in defending there is one rule of overriding significance, namely to *count* declarer's points, shape and tricks. Your mind should be fixed on one goal, beating the contract. The expert defender tries to place the missing cards in a way, consistent with the available clues, that will allow him to defeat declarer. All other guidelines, such as 'second hand plays low', and 'return partner's suit' take a back seat.

When you first start counting you will inevitably find it slow and tiring. Be patient. Like with any other skill you will speed up with practice, and you will soon learn to recognise those hands where counting is likely to bring reward. Our book only really scratches the surface of this vital topic, but we hope to, at the very least, open up new horizons and interest you in further study.

Counting Points

In the hand below partner leads the ♡Q, dummy taking the ♡A. Declarer calls for dummy's ◇J, covered by your ◇Q and taken by declarer's ◇A, and at trick 3 you capture the ◇10 continuation with the ◇K. How should you proceed?

♠ Q 8 3
♡ A 7 2
◇ J 5
♣ A K Q 10 4

Love all
Dealer: North

♠ K J 4 2
♡ 8 6 3
◇ K Q 2
♣ 8 7 5

SOUTH	WEST	NORTH	EAST
		1♣	No
1NT	No	3NT	No
No	No		

The crucial clue comes with South's 1NT response, which shows 8–10 points opposite a 1♣ opening bid. You know he started with the ◇A. He also has the ♡K, as partner's ♡Q lead denied the ♡K. That already makes 7 points. *He cannot hold the ♠A also.* Therefore you can switch with confidence to the ♠2. Indeed if declarer can be relied upon not to bid 1NT over 1♣ with a 4-card major you can be sure of collecting 4 spade tricks to defeat the contract.

There is also another way of looking at this problem that leads you to the same conclusion. Declarer has 8 top tricks (the ♡ A K, ◇A and 5 clubs) and if he did have the ♠A that would give him 9 tricks. You shouldn't waste energy worrying that the contract might be laydown. There is no room for pessimism when defending. Declarer's play is also consistent with his searching for a ninth trick in the diamond suit.

Note the wealth of clues available. Sherlock Holmes would have made a wonderful defender, searching out every scrap of information.

Counting points is particularly likely to bring reward when one of the hidden hands has made a limit bid, or has passed early in the auction and shown up with honour cards.

Counting Shape

In the next example your ◇2 lead is taken by dummy's ◇A. Trumps are drawn (East having two) ending in dummy, and the ◇9 is ruffed. South then exits with a club. You allow East to win this with his ♣K, and he returns a club to your ♣Q. The ♣A wins the next trick and you must find a safe exit.

	♠ J 8 4 3	*North South Game*		
	♡ A 10 9 3	*Dealer:* North		
	◇ A 9	SOUTH	WEST	NORTH	EAST
	♣ 9 6 4			No	3◇
♠ 7 2		3♠	No	4♠	No
♡ Q 8 6	N	No	No		
◇ Q 6 2	W E				
♣ A Q 7 5 2	S				

At first glance it seems as though you have been endplayed. Playing a minor suit will give declarer a ruff-and-discard, while opening up the heart suit can only damage you. Try counting declarer's exact shape. He started with 5 spades, 3 clubs and a singleton diamond. Therefore he must have 4 hearts. A ruff and discard will do him no good whatsoever, simply allowing him to dispose of his fourth heart from hand or dummy. Let him do his own work in the heart suit. The good news is that if partner has ♡ J x the contract is doomed. Even if declarer has the ♡K and ♡J, at least make him guess. Declarer's hand is:

♠ A K Q 10 5   ♡ K 5 4 2   ◇ 4   ♣ J 10 3

Incidentally, there is a tiny, though certainly not conclusive clue that South's hearts won't be brilliant. With ♡ K J x x he might have preferred a take-out double to the 3♠ overcall.

To many defenders it is a cardinal rule that you never give declarer a ruff-and-discard. Systematic counting makes rigid rules obsolete.

Counting Tricks

How do you plan to defeat declarer's no-trump game in our next hand? West leads the ♡2 to dummy's ♡6 and you win the trick with the ♡A.

♠ A 2
♡ K J 6
◇ A K Q 10 3
♣ J 9 3

Game all
Dealer: North

SOUTH	WEST	NORTH	EAST
		1◇	No
1NT	No	3NT	No
No	No		

♠ 7 5 3
♡ A 5 3
◇ 6 4 2
♣ K Q 10 4

You can count declarer for 8 tricks: the ♠A, 2 hearts and 5 diamonds. He could easily have the ♣A, after all he must have something for the 1NT response, but such thoughts are defeatist.

Unless partner has the ♣A the defence will be helpless, so assume he has it. In that case you should switch to the ♣4, in case declarer has:

♠ K Q 10   ♡ 10 9 4   ◇ J 8 5   ♣ 8 7 6 5

Note that not only does counting tricks show you the necessity of a club switch, but, provided you have an open mind, you may also decide that the standard lead (in this case the ♣K) may not be best. Tables of correct leads from combinations shouldn't be a substitute for logical thinking.

Ignoring the Guide-lines

In the hand below West leads the ◇5, dummy playing low and your ◇Q winning the trick. You return the ◇9, South's ◇J holding the trick, and West follows suit with the ◇4. Dummy is entered with the ♠A and the ♡4 comes next. How should you defend?

♠ A K Q J 5 2
♡ 6 4
◇ K 6 2
♣ 9 7

	Love all		
	Dealer: North		
SOUTH	WEST	NORTH	EAST
		1♠	No
2NT	No	3NT	No
No	No		

♠ 10 8 6
♡ A 9 2
◇ Q 9 3
♣ Q 8 5 2

On this hand we are going to see another of the guide-lines become irrelevant. Partner led the ◇5 and followed with the ◇4. This shows a 5-card suit. In that case you can defeat the contract by rising with the ♡A and playing your last diamond. If you fail to take your ♡A declarer will make the ♡K and run for home as he would then have 9 tricks. He has:

♠ 9 7 4   ♡ K Q J 5   ◇ J 8   ♣ A J 4 3

There is no point in getting this wrong and then whining about the need for second hand to play low. When counting provides the evidence that one line of play will defeat the contract, no other argument is relevant.

Note also that even if you personally would prefer 2♣ to 2NT with the South hand, you have to cope with the real world where opponents do make slightly dubious bids. Partner had given you conclusive evidence of the diamond layout, and you should trust partner rather than opponents.

Inferences

For our final example your opponents are reliable players. You cash the ♠A against 6♡, East and South following with insignificant low spades. How should you continue?

	♠ 6 2			
	♡ 6 4			
	♢ 9 5 3			
	♣ A K Q J 7 3			

East West Game
Dealer: South

SOUTH	WEST	NORTH	EAST
2♣	No	3♣	No
4NT	No	5♢	No
6♡	No	No	No

♠ A K J 9 8 4
♡ 8 5 3 2
♢ 8 6
♣ 6

Does it appear natural to continue with a second spade? You don't really expect the ♠K to win do you? Surely declarer wouldn't have used Blackwood with 2 losing spades. Equally Blackwood would be inappropriate with a void in clubs, so declarer may well have:

♠ 3   ♡ A K Q J 10 9 7   ♢ A K Q 10   ♣ 8

The winning defence is to switch to a club, cutting declarer off from dummy's suit. Of course he can still fulfil his contract by finessing the ♢10 immediately, but he has no reason to do that.

The stronger and more reliable your opponents are, the more you can deduce from their actions.

Quiz 18

1)

	♠ Q 3 2	*Love all*			
	♡ K 10 6	*Dealer:* South			
	♢ 9 6 5	SOUTH	WEST	NORTH	EAST
	♣ A J 5 3	2NT	No	3NT	No

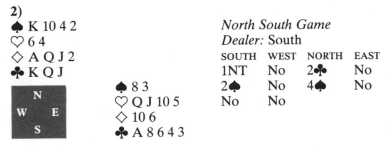

♠ 10 5 4
♡ A 5
♢ A J 4 3 2
♣ 9 6 2

SOUTH WEST NORTH EAST
2NT No 3NT No
No No

You lead the ♢3 to East's ♢10 and South's ♢Q. Declarer switches to the ♡2 at trick 2. Plan the defence.

2)

♠ K 10 4 2   *North South Game*
♡ 6 4   *Dealer:* South
♢ A Q J 2
♣ K Q J

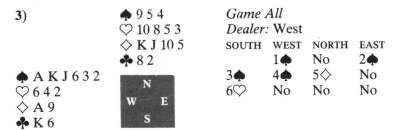

♠ 8 3
♡ Q J 10 5
♢ 10 6
♣ A 8 6 4 3

SOUTH	WEST	NORTH	EAST
1NT	No	2♣	No
2♠	No	4♠	No
No	No		

West leads the ♣2. How should you defend?

3)

♠ 9 5 4   *Game All*
♡ 10 8 5 3   *Dealer:* West
♢ K J 10 5

♣ 8 2

♠ A K J 6 3 2
♡ 6 4 2
♢ A 9
♣ K 6

SOUTH	WEST	NORTH	EAST
	1♠	No	2♠
3♣	4♠	5♢	No
6♡	No	No	No

Your ♠A lead against South's heart slam is ruffed and South leads the ♢4 at trick 2. How should West defend?

4)

♠ K 7 2
♡ 9 6 3 2
♢ K Q 7
♣ K 5 4

Game all
Dealer: South

SOUTH	WEST	NORTH	EAST
1♡	No	3♡	No
6♡	No	No	No

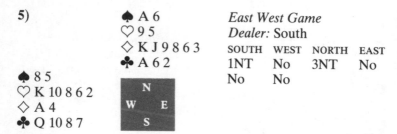

♠ 9 8 4 3
♡ A
♢ A 9 6 3 2
♣ 9 8 7

West leads the ♣Q against 6♡. Dummy's ♣K wins the trick and declarer calls for the ♢7. Should East play the ♢A?

5)

♠ A 6
♡ 9 5
♢ K J 9 8 6 3
♣ A 6 2

East West Game
Dealer: South

SOUTH	WEST	NORTH	EAST
1NT	No	3NT	No
No	No		

♠ 8 5
♡ K 10 8 6 2
♢ A 4
♣ Q 10 8 7

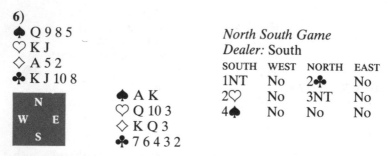

West leads the ♡6 to East's ♡A and East returns the ♡Q. How should West defend?

6)

♠ Q 9 8 5
♡ K J
♢ A 5 2
♣ K J 10 8

North South Game
Dealer: South

SOUTH	WEST	NORTH	EAST
1NT	No	2♣	No
2♡	No	3NT	No
4♠	No	No	No

♠ A K
♡ Q 10 3
♢ K Q 3
♣ 7 6 4 3 2

West leads a trump to your ♠K. How do you continue?

Answers to Quizzes

Answers to quiz 1

1) (a) Pass. While a 4–4 spade fit might be superior to 1NT, you cannot afford to investigate with Stayman because any response other than 2♠ would fix you.

(b) 2◇ [S]. A 2♡ response to Stayman would leave you floundering.

(c) 2♣ [C]. Safe this time, since you can happily pass any response including 2◇.

(d) Pass. If you try 2♣ and pass a 2◇ response you might be in a 4–2 fit if opener has 3–3–2–5 shape.

(e) 2♣. If opener responds 2◇ you can sign off in 2♡, otherwise you can pass his response. Don't settle for a heart fit with no guarantee of a combined 8-card holding when you can investigate a 4–4 spade fit.

(f) 2♣. Forget the clubs. If opener responds 2♠ show appreciation of your distribution by raising to 4♠, otherwise your second bid will be 2NT.

(g) 3♠ [GF]. This time you are looking for a 5–3 fit.

(h) 2♣. Difficult. You are not strong enough for the game-forcing 3♠. Equally you are too strong for a 2♠ sign-off. At present you have no bid available to make a game invitation while showing *five* spades. The best compromise is to test whether opener has four spades, otherwise try 2NT.

(j) 2♣, with a view to playing in 4♠ if partner has four. He may be less balanced than you.

2) (a) (i) 2NT [I] over 2◇. Game try.

(ii) 2NT [I] over 2♡. Game try, showing four spades (otherwise you wouldn't have used Stayman).

(iii) 3♠ [I] over 2♠. Game try, confirming that a 4–4 fit has been uncovered.

(b) (i) 3NT. (ii) 3NT. (iii) 4♠. The same logic applies as in part (a) except that this time you are strong enough to insist on game

3) (a) (i) and (ii) 3NT. This time you are maximum so accept the invitations. Note that you lose nothing by trying

3NT when partner raises to 3♡. If you show your 4–3–3–3 shape partner might have similar shape and judge that the nine trick game is better, otherwise he can retreat to 4♡.
(b) (i) 3♠ [S]. Holding both majors yourself you know a 4–4 fit exists immediately you hear partner's 2♣ bid. You dutifully respond your lowest suit. If he denies interest in hearts by bidding no-trumps, he must have been looking for spades. Being minimum you should not raise to game if he only invites.
    (ii) Pass.
(c) (i) 4♠ [S]. (ii) 4♡ [S]. As (b), except that with a maximum you accept any invitation to game.

Answers to quiz 2

2) (a) 2♡. Simple preference, showing 6–9 points.
(b) 2♡. You don't have the ten points required to make a constructive continuation. Neither do you have a good enough spade suit to rebid 2♠. Therefore you must choose between partner's suits.
(c) Pass. You have no sensible alternative.
(d) 3♡ [L]. Jump preference. 3-card support, 10–12 points.
(e) 2NT [L]. 10–12 HCP and a diamond guard.
(f) 2♠ [L]. Good suit, weak hand.
(g) 2NT [L]. Don't use the fourth suit when you have a perfectly descriptive natural bid available.
(h) 2♡ [L]. Simple preference.
(j) 2♢ [C]. The fourth suit, showing at least the values for 2NT but with no natural bid available.

2) (a) (i) 3NT [GF]. A better than minimum opening bid with at least one spade stopper.
    (ii) 3♠ [GF]. The fourth suit at the 3-level is game-forcing.
(b) (i) 4♣ [GF], suggesting a strong 1–5–4–3 pattern.
    (ii) 3NT [GF], with a bit to spare.
(c) (i) 3♢ [NF]. Minimum and usually 5–5 shape.
    (ii) 3♢ [GF]. Expectancy is a 5–5 pattern.

Answers to quiz 3

1)   (i)   Not a reverse. Preference bid is 2◇. Not forcing.
    (ii) Reverse. Preference bid is 3♣. Forcing for one round because responder changed suit at the one level.
    (iii) Not a reverse. Preference bid is 2♡. Not forcing in standard Acol.
    (iv) Reverse. Preference bid is 3♡. Game-forcing because responder changed suit at the two-level.
    (v) Reverse. Preference bid is 3♠. Game-forcing.
    (vi) This is a jump shift [GF], not a reverse.

2)   (a) Open 1◇ and rebid 2◇ [L]. Too weak for a 2♡ rebid.
    (b) Open 1◇ and rebid 2♡ [F1R]. If responder makes a minimum rebid you will pass.
    (c) Open 1◇ and rebid 2♡ [F1R]. This time you will continue to game over any rebid by responder.
    (d) Open 1♡ and rebid 2◇ [WR] [NF].
    (e) Open 1♡ and rebid 2◇ [WR] [NF]. This hand is better than (d) but not strong enough for 3◇ [GF].
    (f) Open 1♡ and rebid 3◇ [GF], showing 19–20 points.

3)   (a) 2NT [NF]. 6–8 points after the reverse.
    (b) 3NT [GF]. Don't rebid 2NT [NF] and risk a pass.
    (c) 2♠ [NF]. Good suit, minimum response.
    (d) 3♠ [GF]. Good suit. Any jump continuation by responder after opener's reverse is game-forcing.
    (e) 3◇ [NF]. Simple preference.
    (f) 4◇ [GF]. Game-forcing.

Answers to quiz 4

1)   (a) Open 1NT [L]. 12–14 HCP and balanced.
    (b) Open 1♡, the lower of two touching 4-card suits, with a balanced hand too strong to open 1NT. Raise a 1♠ response to 3♠ or rebid 2NT (15–16 points) if responder bids a minor suit at the two level.
    (c) Open 1♡. Raise 1♠ to 4♠ or rebid 3NT (17–19 points) if responder changes suit at the two level.
    (d) Open 1NT. Don't let your weak doubleton worry you.
    (e) Open 1♡, the higher of non-touching 4-card suits,

with a balanced hand too strong to open 1NT. Rebid 1NT (15–16 points) over a 1♠ response or 2NT (15–16 points) over a 2♢ response. If the response is 2♣ you can rebid 2NT to show your balanced shape, or maybe raise to 3♣.

(f)   Open 1♡. Rebid 3NT over any response.

2)   (a)   Open 1♡. With a black suit singleton open the middle of three touching 4-card suits. Rebid 2♢ over 2♣.

(b)   Open 1♢ and rebid 2♣ over 1♠.

(c)   Open 1♣. With a red suit singleton open the suit below the singleton. Rebid 1♡ over 1♢.

3)   (i)   5 spades.   (ii) 5 spades.

(iii)   A balanced hand with perhaps only 4 spades.

(iv)   5 hearts.

(v)   4 hearts if exactly 4–4–4–1 shape (singleton club). Otherwise 5 hearts.

(vi)   5 hearts. Any reverse guarantees 5 cards in the first suit.

4)   (a)   Open 1♡. Rebid 2♣ over 1♠, or 2♡ over 2♢.

(b)   Open 1♡. Rebid 2♣ over 1♠, or reverse into 3♣ [GF] over 2♢.

(c)   Open 1♡. Jump to 3♣ [GF] over 1♠, or reverse into 3♣ [GF] over 2♢.

(d)   Open 1♣. Rebid 2♣ [L] over 1♡. If the response is 1♠ it is better to raise to 2♠ [L] with good 3-card support than rebid your wretched club suit. A single raise of partner's major doesn't guarantee 4-card support. You are too weak to reverse into 2♢.

(e)   Open 1♣. Reverse into 2♢ [F1R] over 1♡ or 1♠.

(f)   Open 1♣. Stronger than (e) but you must still start by reversing into 2♢ over 1♡ or 1♠. Eventually you will insist on game.

(g)   Open 1♡. Rebid 2♣ over 1♠, or 2♡ over 2♢.

(h)   Open 1♡. Rebid 2♣ over 1♠, or reverse into 3♣ over 2♢.

(j)   Open 1♡. Jump to 3♣ over 1♠, or reverse into 3♣ over 2♢.

Answers to quiz 5

1)   (a)   1♠. Don't raise 1♡ to 2♡ with only 3-card support if you have four spades.

    (b)   2♡ [L]. If opener rebids 2NT [I] you should pass.

    (c)   1NT [L]. 4–3–3–3 pattern, the only time you prefer a 1NT response to raising a major with 3-card support.

2)   (a)   Pass. If you are in a 4–3 fit there will be some ruffing value in the short hand.

    (b)   3NT [GF]. Partner will correct to 4♡ if he has 4 hearts.

    (c)   4♡ [S]. At least a 5–3 fit.

3)   (a)   3♡ [S]. 4-card heart support but a minimum 2♡ response.

    (b)   Pass. Opener has 17–18 balanced points.

    (c)   3NT [S]. As with (b) but this time you have better values.

4)   (a)   1NT [L]. Don't respond 2♢ [F1R] which might force a 2♡ rebid, and then pass.

    (b)   2♢. You can continue with 2NT over a 2♡ rebid.

    (c)   1♠. With a hand worth only one bid, choose the major.

    (d)   2♣. Then bid spades next time.

    (e)   1♠. Not 3NT with a 4-card spade suit.

    (f)   3NT [L]. 4–3–3–3 shape. Denies four spades.

    (g)   2♣, then 3NT next time.

    (h)   2NT [L]. 11–12 HCP and the perfect shape.

    (j)   2NT. If partner has five hearts he can test whether you have 3-card support by bidding 3♣ or 3♢, even if the minor has only three cards. If he does rebid 3♣ or 3♢ you should resist the temptation to support the minor, instead rebidding 3NT to deny 3-card heart support.

5)   (a)   1♡. The lower of two 4-card suits. Opener will rebid 1♠ if he has four spades.

    (b)   1♠. The higher of two 5-card suits. This allows you to introduce your heart suit after a no-trump rebid without reversing.

    (c)   1♠. Prefer to bid your 4-card major rather than to give immediate minor support.

Answers to quiz 6

1)   (a)   Open 1♠ in any position.

(b)   You are two weak to open as dealer, but the urgency of encouraging a spade lead makes a third in hand 1♠ reasonable.

(c)   Pass in any position. If you chose to open it would have to be 1♠, and you hardly want a spade lead.

(d)   Open 1NT in any position.

(e)   Pass in any position. Too many isolated honours and no intermediate cards (10s and 9s).

(f)   Pass as dealer. Open 1♣ in third seat. You can rebid 1♠ over 1♢, or pass a 1♡ response. Logically a change of suit after a third-in-hand opening cannot be forcing as responder cannot have opening values.

2)   (a)   6♠ is sensible. The hands seem to fit well, with ♣ Q 7 an excellent holding in partner's side suit. It wouldn't be practical to investigate a grand slam.

(b)   Pass. A singleton in partner's suit will hardly help you establish it, and you have too much of your strength in the red suits.

(c)   4NT. The hands don't seem to fit especially well, but you are strong enough to make a slam provided he has 3 aces. He can hardly have less than 2 aces, so the five level should be safe.

3)   (a)   4♠. All your honour cards are in his suits, so the hands fit beautifully.

(b)   3♠. Three small cards in his second suit are not helpful, and your ♣Q and ♡Q are likely to be useless.

(c)   4♠. Your diamond holding is disappointing, but everything else is good. You have a maximum for 2♠, excellent trumps, and any ace is likely to be helpful.

Answers to quiz 7

1)   (a)   Pass. Too weak for a 1NT overcall. It would be foolish to double because if partner bids 1♠ you may be in a 4–2 fit. An attempted rescue to 1NT would then show 19–20 HCP, compounding your felony.

(b)   1NT [L]. Balanced 16–18 HCP and a diamond guard.

(c)   Double, and then give a single raise in partner's choice of suit. This is consistent with a hand that would open the bidding and then give a jump raise.

(d)   Double, then rebid 1NT over 1♡ or 1♠ (19–20 HCP) or rebid 2NT over 2♣ (19–21 HCP).

(e)   2♡. 14–17 HCP and a good 6-card suit.

(f)   Double, and then bid spades at the lowest possible level, showing a hand that is too strong for a 1♠ overcall, but lacking a sixth spade for 2♠.

(g)   Double, then rebid 2NT over 1♡ or 1♠ (21–23 HCP) or rebid 3NT over 2♣ (22 or more HCP).

(h)   Double, and then jump in hearts, showing a hand too strong for an immediate 2♡ jump overcall.

(j)   Pass. Despite your strength you have no intelligent bid to make. It is usually wise to pass when so much of your strength is concentrated in the enemy suit.

2)

(i)   (a)   Pass. Partner has a good 6-card suit. Attempting to rescue will make matters worse.

(b)   4♡ [S]. You seem to have an outstanding fit and might make game with very few points.

(c)   3♡ [I]. You want to try game unless he is minimum.

(ii)   (a)   Pass. Obvious.

(b)   Pass. It is unlikely now that anyone will double.

(c)   Pass. The poor fit makes game unlikely.

(iii)   (a)   Pass. Partner might not be balanced. Hope he can beat 1NT doubled by himself.

(b)   2♠. This time the spades are self-supporting, and you don't fancy defending 1NT doubled if he leads the inevitable club.

(c)   Pass. You should pick up a useful penalty.

(iv)   (a), (b) and (c)   2♠ [S]. Playing 1NT doubled won't be much fun if North leads out a solid club suit. Note that 2♣ isn't Stayman if 1NT is doubled.

3)

(i)   (a)   3♡ [L]. One level higher after the double.

(b)   1NT [L]. As if North had passed.

(c)   2♣ [F1R]. Again the double makes no difference.

(ii)   (a)   2♡ [L]. Ignoring the overcall.

(b)   1NT [L]. You have the spades stopped.

(c)   2♣ [F1R]. Bid naturally.

(iii) (a)   2♥ [L]. Not strong enough to double.

(b) and (c)   Double, for penalties. Your side has the majority of HCP. That may not guarantee beating a suit contract for which shape and playing strength are crucial, but it is usually a good guide to your chances of beating a no-trump contract.

(iv)   (a)   2♥ [L]. No difference.

(b)   Pass or 2♦. Nasty! You don't like passing with nine HCP, but neither do you like bidding this revolting diamond suit at the two level.

(c)   Double, for penalties as partner has already bid.

(v)   (a)   3♥ [L]. Borrow a HCP or two rather than conceal your heart support.

(b)   With your spade honours well placed the overbid of 2NT [L] is probably best, though pass and double are reasonable alternatives.

(c)   Pass (too strong) or 3♣ [F1R] (too weak). A brute!

(vi)   (a)   1♥ is better than 1NT. Don't forget West probably has four hearts and a singleton diamond.

(b)   2♣. Ugh! You are really too strong for this bid but 3♣ on this horrid suit is a distortion. 1NT, which shows your strength better, is an alternative but your diamond holding opposite a singleton will hardly provide satisfactory cover for a no-trump contract.

(c)   3♣. No problem this time.

(vii) (a)   Pass. Not 1NT which shows 9–12 HCP.

(b) and (c)   2♠. Mild game suggestions.

(viii) West is a protecting hand and may be 3 HCP weaker than normal, so you underbid by 3 HCP.

(a)   1♥   (b) and (c)   2♣

(ix)   Again West is a protective hand.

(a), (b) and (c)   All pass.

(x)   West is a protective hand but:

(a)   Pass.

(b)   2♠. Stretch a bit in competition to show your fit.

(c)   Double, for penalties! Sadly they will probably run to 2♦ and you will then try 2♠.

4)

(i)   (a)   Double, for take-out.

(b)   2♠. They have a heart fit. You may have a spade fit. If the points are split 20–20 you should be contesting the part-score as it is quite likely that 2♡ and 2♠ both make.

(c)   Pass. You have too much of your strength in their suit to compete.

(ii)   (a)   Double for take-out looks risky, but is not unreasonable. If partner bids hearts you can bid 2♠ offering a choice between the other suits. Partner cannot imagine you have a strong hand (as would normally be the case if you double and then bid on) because you passed first time. This shows how aggressive your stance can be in the protective position. Of course pass is a reasonable alternative.

(b)   2♠. As with (i) (b).

(c)   Pass. You have too much of your strength in clubs.

Answers to quiz 8

1)   You have 3 spades missing and only one card greater than the K, so finesse the ♠Q.

2)   You have just 2 spades missing so rise with the ♠A, playing for a 1–1 break.

3)   Take trick 4 in dummy and lead the ♠2, finessing the ♠Q if East plays low. You will succeed in avoiding a trump loser if East has the ♠K doubleton or singleton. Note that leading the ♠J costs a trick if East has the ♠K singleton and won't work if East has ♠ K x x because East will cover the ♠J with the ♠K, promoting the ♠10 or ♠9 for the defenders.

4)   Take trick 4 in dummy and lead the ♠J. If East plays low, run it. You avoid a trump loser is East has the ♠K tripleton, doubleton or singleton. The alternative play of a low spade from dummy to the ♠Q is not good enough if East has ♠ K x x because there is no further entry to dummy to repeat the finesse.

Answers to quiz 9

1)   With 7 top tricks, you can develop enough from diamonds or clubs, but you cannot afford to relinquish the lead. Your best chance is to take the ♠A and cash the ◇ A K. If the

◇Q falls you are home, otherwise you can fall back on the club finesse.

When you appear to have a choice of finesses for your contract the following guide-line is helpful. *Start by cashing the top cards in the suit where they are more likely to crash the missing honour, then if unsuccessful take the finesse in the other suit.* Here you are far more likely to find the ◇Q doubleton than the ♣K singleton.

2) Before committing yourself to the heart finesse it cannot cost to see if the ◇K will provide a heart discard. Therefore win the ♡A, draw trumps ending in your hand, and lead the ◇6.

3) and 4)

(i) and (ii)   With either of these hands a diamond or club lead allows you to test all your options for the vital thirteenth trick. Therefore you would cash your clubs, test the diamond suit for a favourable break, and if that fails enter your hand with the ♠A, discard the diamond loser on the ♠K and finesse dummy's ♡Q.

(iii)   Percentages don't matter here. West won't have led from the ♡K against a grand slam so rise with your ♡A and hope you can make 4 diamond tricks.

(iv)   With the only entry to your hand removed at trick 1 you must cash your second spade trick now.

Playing (3) you should prefer the heart finesse (50%) to a 3–3 diamond break (36%). Discard the ◇7.

Playing (4) you should hope for a 3–2 diamond break (68%). Discard the ♡Q on the ♠K.

Answers to quiz 10

1) (i)   In the grand slam you need 5 club tricks. Win the ♠A, cash the ♣A, return to your hand with a diamond and run the ♣J. You will succeed if the ♣Q is singleton, or if West has the ♣Q doubleton or tripleton.

(ii)   The only possible problem in 6NT is if clubs break 5–0. You are unlikely to succeed if West has ♣ Q 9 8 7 6, but if East has this holding, careful play should ensure success. Take the ♠A and lead a low club towards the ♣J.

2) You have 12 top tricks, so what can go wrong? Although West probably has only 7 spades for his pre-empt, it is not impossible that he has an 8-card suit, in which case there is the danger of East ruffing your ♠A at trick 1, reducing your trick total to 11. However, if you duck trick 1, nothing can harm your ♠A. Ruff a spade continuation at trick 2 and draw trumps.

3) (i) This is very unpleasant. You can only take the ♣A, cash the ♠ A K, and start playing diamonds. If the ◇J falls singleton or doubleton you can complete drawing trumps, enter dummy with the ◇9 and discard a club on the ♡A. Otherwise, if the same defender has 3 diamonds and 3 trumps you can cash the ◇ A K Q, ruff the ◇2 and discard your club loser on dummy's ♡A.
    (ii) Take the ♣A, draw trumps and play the ◇A followed by the ◇10. If a defender takes the ◇J your ◇9 will give you an entry to the ♡A. Otherwise, there will be no diamond loser.

4) (i) Ruff the ♠A in dummy, hopefully draw trumps in 3 rounds and cash your winners.
    (ii) In 6♡ you can afford a trump loser, but if there is a trump to be lost you want to lose it while you still have a trump in dummy to cope with a spade continuation. Therefore trump the ♠A and immediately duck a trump.

Answers to quiz 11

1) This looks like giving you 13 comfortable tricks, but beware. What if East has ♠ J x x x and a singleton diamond? If you play off 3 top trumps and turn your attention to diamonds he will ruff and lead hearts through your vulnerable holding. West is the safe hand: you don't mind losing a trick to him so win the ♣A and finesse your ♠10.

2) Having won trick 1 cheaply with the ♡10, you must consider which finesse to take first. Diamonds are the longer suit, but if you lose to East's ◇K he will persevere with hearts, and if West subsequently gains the lead with the ♠K, 3 heart tricks and 2 kings might defeat you. At present West is the safe hand, unable to attack hearts, so you want to enter dummy in order to finesse spades. It is dangerous

138

to use clubs as the defenders might switch their attack to clubs. That leaves you with the surprising but foolproof solution of entering dummy with the ♢A and finessing spades. You never take the diamond finesse!

3) You have been fortunate to avoid a heart lead. As it is West is the safe hand, which means that if the diamond finesse is working you don't need to take it. Best play is to try a diamond to dummy's ♢A, gaining spectacularly if East has the ♢K singleton. Of course, if East has the guarded ♢K and switches to a heart, and West holds the ♡A, you are helpless.

4) This contract is laydown, provided you can resist trying to make extra tricks from diamonds. Take the ♡K, making West the safe hand, enter dummy with the ♣Q, and finesse your ♠J. If West switches to a diamond rise with dummy's ♢A and cash your nine top tricks.

Answers to quiz 12

1) You have plenty of winners, but with only 7 trumps there is a danger that you may lose trump control. Ruff the ♡Q and try the ♠Q from your hand. If a defender takes the ♠K now you can ruff a heart continuation in dummy. If the ♠Q is allowed to win, enter dummy with the ♢A and finesse the ♠J. If this wins cash the ♠A and play your minor suit winners. You will only be defeated on a 5–1 spade break, or a 4–2 break if West has the ♠K and is awake enough to duck the ♠Q at trick 4.

2) Can you make your contract if spades break 4–2? Declining to trump the second heart won't help as the defenders can switch to diamonds. Instead ruff the heart continuation and duck a trump, losing the trick while you still have a trump in dummy to cope with a further heart force.

3) If you cash 2 trump tricks and they break 2–2 you will comfortably make 11 tricks. If they break 3–1 a defender gaining the lead can draw a third round, holding you to 9 tricks. Therefore take the ♣A, cash just the ♠K and duck a diamond to set up your cross-ruff.

4) This is nasty. You cannot duck 4 heart tricks, so you will be forced to ruff with the 4-card holding. Best play is to ruff at

trick 3, draw just 2 rounds of trumps and start cashing your diamonds. If a defender trumps and persists with a fourth heart you can ruff, cross to your hand with the ♣K, draw the last trump with the ♠10, enter dummy with the ♣A and persevere with diamonds.

Answers to quiz 13

1) Win the ♠A, draw trumps, cash the ♠ K Q and ♣A and exit with a club. The defenders will now have to concede a ruff-and-discard or play hearts. Suppose West leads the ♡4. Play low from dummy, East winning the ♡Q. Whoever has the ♡K, East is now endplayed.

2) Take the ♣A, draw trumps, eliminate hearts, cash the ◇K and lead a second diamond, playing dummy's ◇10 if West follows low. East is endplayed.

3) You would like to eliminate spades and diamonds before endplaying West with a trump. Sadly, you don't have enough entries to fully eliminate diamonds, but a partial elimination might be worthwhile. Take the ♠K, cash the ♡A and the ◇A, and ruff a diamond. Re-enter dummy with the ♠A and ruff another diamond. Now give West his ♡K. If West started with only 3 diamonds he will be endplayed. Even if he can exit safely with a diamond you have lost nothing as you can subsequently enter dummy with the ♡9 to take the club finesse yourself.

4) Win the ◇A and drive out the ♣A. West perseveres with a second diamond, won by your ◇Q. Cash the clubs and the ◇K, revealing that West started with 4 diamonds. Plan to extract West's exit cards by cashing the ♡ A K, and throw him in with the ◇4, forcing him to concede a trick to your ♠K.

Answers to quiz 14

1) Trump the third heart. You must now avoid losing two trump tricks. West is marked with the ♠A on the bidding so leading up to the ♠K is guaranteed to fail. You must hope that East has a holding like ♠ J 10 x. Enter dummy

with the ♢A and lead the ♠3, inserting your ♠9 if East plays low.

2) West has 9 clubs, and the only explanation for East's failure to ruff your ♣A is that he has no trumps. You therefore know West has 12 black cards. Which red singleton has he? Well, if he has no diamonds you are doomed as you have no future entry to dummy to take a diamond finesse, so assume he has a singleton diamond and no heart. While his diamond could be the ♢J, it is 4 times more likely to be a low card so you should finesse the ♢10 immediately.

3) Having shown 8 points in diamonds West must have the ♡A, or the ♣K, but not both.
    (i)   If you are in 2♠ the only danger to your contract is if East has the ♣K, so place him with this card. That gives West the ♡A, so try the ♡J from your hand.
    (ii) If you are in 3♠ your only chance is for West to hold the ♣K, so place him with this card. This means East must hold the ♡A, so rise with your ♡K.

Answers to quiz 15

1) With 5 trump tricks, 5 clubs (assuming no 4–0 break) and two aces what can go wrong? The club suit will be blocked if either defender has ♣ J x x. The solution is elegant. Draw trumps, ending in dummy, and throw the offending ♣9 on the ♢8. This is actually a winner-on-loser play.

2) The ♡7 lead suggests the heart finesse may be wrong, but you will still succeed unless West has the ♢K and ♢Q (which is unlikely as he might then have chosen to lead the ♢K). Take the ♡A, draw trumps, enter dummy with the ♢A and discard the ♡6 on the ♢J. West wins and perseveres with hearts but you ruff, cross to dummy with the ♣A and take a ruffing finesse in diamonds to discard a losing club.

3) It looks so natural to ruff the ♣Q, but that leaves you struggling to avoid 2 diamond losers. Better play is to discard the ♢2 from dummy at trick 1. East wins the ♣A but your ♣K later allows you to dispose of the second diamond loser.

4) You certainly have 10 winners, but if you take an unsuc-cessful diamond finesse East can pierce your vulnerable

club holding, resulting in 4 immediate losers. To ensure your contract rise with the ♢A, draw trumps, cash the ♡A and take a ruffing heart finesse, discarding a *diamond* if East doesn't cover the ♡Q with the ♡K. West might win the ♡K, but he is the safe hand, unable to threaten your club holding.

Answers to quiz 16

1)   (i)   The ♠5. Not the ♠K which will block the suit if partner has ♠ J x or ♠ A x.
  (ii)   The ♠K. Set up one quick trick and maybe give partner a ruff.

2)   (i)   The ♣8 (middle card from three small). Defend passively. North/South don't have much to spare and the major suits are lying badly for them.
  (ii)   The ♢3. North has 4 spades, South has 4 hearts. This time the cards seem to be lying well for them and North is unlimited in strength.

3)   (i)   The ♡J. With such excellent spades sitting after South, defend passively.
  (ii)   The ♠A. Clearly a spade lead is right, and the ♠A avoids two losers if one defender has ♠ K x and the other ♠ 10 9 x x, because you can continue with the ♣6 at trick 2. The ♢A gives you the necessary entry.

4)   (i)   The ♡8. Prefer the longer red suit holding. Your 'help' may not be brilliant, but a tripleton will help him set up his suit more than a doubleton.
  (ii)   The ♠2. The suit which requires least help from partner. Leading from an unsupported jack is not very constructive. The ♡8, hoping to lead passively through dummy's suit, is a possible alternative.

5)   (i)   The ♡3, aiming for a ruff.
  (ii)   The ♣J. The singleton heart is pointless, because if partner has an entry the slam is going to be defeated whatever happens.

6)   (i)   The ♡3. It sounds as though 5♠ asked South to bid 6♠ with a heart control. Given time no doubt South's hearts will disappear on North's minor suits, so you had better hope your partner has the ♡Q.

(ii)   The ♠A. You have nothing that would suggest that South's minor suit is less solid than he thinks. You need to attack quickly. Leading an ace allows you to see dummy before committing yourself further.

7)   (i)   A heart. North/South seem to have a 5–3 heart fit so you hope partner can ruff this. You will learn in chapter 19 that the lead of an unnecessarily high heart (the ♡8) will be seen by partner as a suit preference signal, requesting him to return a diamond, the higher ranking of the side suits.
(ii)   The ◇A. The fact that South bid 5♣ rather than 3NT suggests he doesn't have the ◇K. Take what is going in diamonds before declarer's losers are discarded on major suit winners.

Answers to quiz 17

1)   The only hope is to make a trump trick and the ♡A. An uppercut may be possible, but you must first cash the ♡A, otherwise South will discard his heart loser when East ruffs with the ♠10. South has:

♠ A K Q 9 4   ♡ 5   ◇ 10 5   ♣ Q J 9 4 3

2)   If East overruffs that will be the last defensive trick. If he discards he will eventually make a trick with the ♠8 if West has the ♠9. South has:

♠ Q 6 5 3 2   ♡ K J 4   ◇ 9 5 2   ♣ A K

3)   West should follow suit with the ♠J, his highest spade to indicate a heart switch. The order of ♠K followed by ♠A is normal, showing East has a third spade, but West badly wants a heart switch while East still has the lead. South has:

♠ 8 5   ♡ K 6 3   ◇ 9 5 4   ♣ A 9 7 4 2

Answers to quiz 18

1)   With South's 2NT opening showing 20–22 points, partner can have at most one jack, so he won't have an entry to lead diamonds through declarer. Your only chance is to hope that South started with ◇ K Q doubleton, in which case

you can rise with your ♡A and cash 4 more diamond tricks. Failure to take the ♡A immediately will allow declarer 9 tricks as he has:

♠ A K J   ♡ Q J 3 2   ◇ K Q   ♣ K Q 10 4

2) Declarer has at least 12 points, dummy has 16 and you have 7. Therefore West has at most 5. The only 5-point holding that will make it possible to defeat the contract involves West having the ♡A, in which case it is essential to switch to the ♡Q at trick 2. Giving your partner an immediate club ruff may be satisfying, but declarer will subsequently be able to discard losing hearts as he has:

♠ A Q 7 5   ♡ K 7 2   ◇ K 7   ♣ 10 9 7 5

3) Declarer has no spades and at most 6 hearts, therefore at least 7 minor suit cards. South's 6♡ bid must be based on good clubs as well as solid hearts, and there is no possibility of dummy's diamonds providing discards for all declarer's clubs, making your ♣K a sure trick. Forget 'second hand low', take your ◇A and exit passively with a spade. South has:

♠ –   ♡ A K Q J 9 7   ◇ 4   ♣ A Q J 10 7 3

4) Don't become too encouraged by your two aces. Ask why declarer didn't use Blackwood. He almost certainly has the other 2 aces and a void diamond. By far your best chance of a side suit trick is in clubs, but don't waste your ◇A on thin air or declarer will be able to discard two clubs on the ◇ K Q. Declarer has:

♠ A Q J   ♡ K Q J 7 5 4   ◇ –   ♣ A 6 3 2

5) West should overtake the ♡Q with his ♡K and persevere with hearts from the top, ensuring the defeat of the contract. If he fails to do this East will have to switch suit, allowing declarer to succeed. South has:

♠ K Q J   ♡ J 7 4 3   ◇ Q 10 5   ♣ K J 9

6) Declarer has at least 12 points, dummy has 14 and you have 14. Partner has nothing! How about shape? South has shown 4 cards in each major suit, so he must be 3–2 in the

minors. Could he have 3 clubs? Surely with a singleton club, 3 trumps and a worthless hand West would have led his club, therefore South has 3 diamonds and 2 clubs. So is there any hope? There might be if West has the ◇10. Switch to the ◇3. If South tries the ◇9, West's ◇10 will force out dummy's ◇A, and if declarer then tries to discard losing diamonds on dummy's winning clubs, West can ruff. South's hand is:

♠ J 10 7 6   ♡ A 6 4 2   ◇ J 9 8   ♣ A Q